MW00461176

Earth Whisperer/ White Chick from Tacoma

By

Anne Marie McNamara

© 2017

For my beloved grandchildren,
you dazzle me with your grace.

What is my Why?

I want to create a better life for the earth. I want to help in the peace process and fill people's hearts with hope. I want to create a safe world of joy and love. I want people to feel safe enough to talk about their deepest fears and their deepest joys. I want people to know themselves and rejoice in themselves. I want to know our own spiritual quest. I want to be comfortable. To let go and be one with my environment and know our own essence. This is not only my dream. It is the dream of many. That is, the inner truth of a desire to help and to be of service in a loving manner.

As you begin to read this book, I thought I would lead with a quote from Albert Einstein, "Reality is merely an illusion, albeit a very persistent one."

Introduction

Hello, m   ⁓ Anne Marie McNamara
and I began a⸱   ing healing therapies that
address both '   t in the 1980s, when I was
working w⸱   ⸱ng people for the county
governm⸱

⸱   , violence, fear, and despair of
many kinds, I fou⸱   ⸱as able to understand and
reach out to these young people, and at the same time
I myself needed to explore and develop the spiritual
strength to continue to help them.

I pursued an education in the physiological
benefits of healing techniques of Eastern, Western,
and Native American spiritual teachings. Later, the
benefits of massage as an important component of my
healing practice became clear to me. It is now 2017
and between that time and this much has happened. I
have taken many courses covering a wide range of
holistic healing therapies. However, until this writing
my story has been semi-hidden. I worried about what

"normal" people including my family would think. I worried that native indigenous people would feel their ways would be disrespected because I am a white chick from Tacoma.   Most indigenous people have always been respectful of my abilities and have honored me in their words and actions. This was nothing more than my own critical fearful thinking. My brain was too stuffed with my own pattern of "be mean to Anne Marie" to hear their words of appreciation. It crippled me for years. Yet I have always believed God or the universe has always wanted us to live joyful lives filled with love for each other. Yes, it is a paradox.

I never read the memo about the importance of self-love. Love your neighbor as yourself meant to me that I needed to love my neighbor most deeply, because it was up to my neighbor to love me best, not me. Loving myself to me was egotistical, self-centered and selfish. It never occurred to me that I could be self-centered, spirit driven, and not use the concept of selfish as a tool of harsh negative judgment. It never occurred to me.

Some of my clients have asked me to share my story. They felt it would be useful to others' personal life paths.

My background is conservative with regards to paranormal phenomena. My father had had a bad experience with a Ouija board. He and his family had gone to Sunday church service. On the return from church, he and some of his siblings immediately decided to play with the Ouija board. As the pointer moved along the board it began to spell out curse words. At that moment, my father decided the board was the work of the devil and refused to have one anywhere near him. We were forbidden to have one in our home and it was frowned upon to use the neighbor's board. It lost its interest for us. Playing outside was much more interesting.

My maternal grandmother, May, was raised with a father that read tea leaves for the neighbors. She was comfortable with paranormal activities. She moved into our house when I was twelve years old. My grandfather, her husband, had died and she sold their house and moved in with us. Well, she had the Ouija board and that was our secret we kept from my father. She kept it in her room under her bed. On occasion, she would pull it out and we would use it. She always said a quick prayer before we used it. I am not sure if my mother knew about it. If she did, she never mentioned it. Neither my mother nor my grandmother agreed with my father about the evils of Ouija boards. How I knew that I am not sure. I just did. Personally, I thought of Ouija boards as interesting but I was not sure how they worked.

The only other type of paranormal activity I remember is trying to do automatic writing. Automatic writing is where someone from another dimension writes through you by way of moving your hand. My sister and I decided to try to do this. We were not patient. We tried a few times with minimal results. It was boring, so we went back to drawing clothes for our paper dolls.

Early Life

I was born in Washington DC under a full moon, the day of summer solstice. My parents were both born and raised in Washington State. My father worked for the government and when he was able to transfer back to Washington State he did. Our family drove cross-country and returned to Tacoma. My mom had grown up in Tacoma. Her mother, born in Minnesota, moved there as a child around 1900. My grandfather, also originally from Minnesota, was hired by Northern Pacific Railway and moved to Tacoma in his late teens. My grandparents did not meet until after World War I. It was love at first sight. They wanted to be married on Valentine's Day but that year it was during Lent so it was not possible, and they married slightly earlier. I think they both felt Valentine's Day was their unofficial anniversary. My dad came to Tacoma in his twenties. He had started working for the government. He had been raised mostly in the Naches area. His parents moved to this side of the Cascade Range about the same time. They lived in Tumwater, next to Olympia. My dad's grandparents were both apple ranchers in the Yakima valley. Our roots run deep in the state of Washington. This is important to help understand my foundation. Tacoma likes homegrown folks and values shared childhood memories through the generations. It was suspicious of outsiders. Most outsiders in my parents' generation came after World War II. Men and women met their prospective mates during the war and returned to Tacoma to raise their families. Tacomans were definitely provincial and had boundaries about outsiders and had opinions about proper behavior and could be quite judgmental. They are also some of the most accepting loving people in the world. People from Tacoma will go the extra mile for you in their hearts. Hence, they cherish their insider's status. Part of being a Tacoman is you feel love. Now you may not have felt liked or understood but LOVE was always there. We are small city family.

I had two main childhood homes growing up in Tacoma, first in a blue-collar neighborhood and later in a white collar upper middle class neighborhood. Both had their wonderment. Both offered parks and nature. Both were considered a safe place to walk to the park. The second home was on a dead-end street. We were the last house on the block, and two of our home's boundaries were a wooded gully or gulch. One time our neighborhood had fifty kids! Years later I went to visit the Japanese neighbors just off our street. They were very glad to see me and offered tea. The husband was ill and not doing well. Still he came out for a short visit. They told me their inside joke was the name they gave our Dead-End Street as The Fertile Valley. Lots of kids!

Our street had many Catholic families. We all attended the local Catholic schools, walked to school, shared some of the same teachers and attended the same functions. As adults, my peers, my sister, and my friends all felt we had group parents. Each parent offered something to the mix. My family loved books and we were the unofficial library for the neighborhood. If you had to write a report, or pick and memorize a poem, head to our house; needed some practical advice, ask another neighbor. One neighborhood mom was the best listener for feelings and romance stories. The dads also played a role. My dad was very parental—guiding us about proper behavior and education. He also made sure each boy had rides to their sport practices and games. Another left work early and drove us for afternoons of lake swimming and ice cream. Another dad offered us warmth, acceptance and a place to watch color TV and eat popcorn on a Friday night. We thought of him as a big teddy bear of comfort. At the time, we took it for granted as normal, but now we realize how special it was. It was not perfect; we had periodic neighborhood squabbles, alcoholism, mental health issues, and typical dysfunctional family patterns. The good news is, one family's issue was not usually another family's issue. We had a broader base to decide what normal was. The parents all accepted the notion that it takes a village to raise a family. The Dead-End Kids still get together as family/friends. My old friends' normal is not my normal. So, what? Love, memories and experience transcend all.

The Life-Changing Event

It was on November 11,1985, at 11 o'clock in the morning, that my life changed forever. At that time, I was a single mother with an amazing teenager. My job was a Juvenile Probation Counselor for King County Youth Services. I was the felon intake worker for our unit and mostly worked with assault cases. My job was to interview the youth and their families, read the police report, gather information to write a report and a recommendation to the court. Most people commented how interesting my job must be. Years later I can appreciate why they said that, but daily reading of police reports takes its toll on one's mind.

My friend Cathy and I were treating ourselves to a latte and a chocolate chip cookie at the B&O Café. It was a holiday and we were "vacationing" for a couple hours. We had become acquainted through my son's and her children's daycare. We were both single parents, divorced, raising our families and attending the University of Washington. Later, we both had demanding careers. We took "vacations" when we could.

I had just finished talking about my son and Cathy was talking about one of her sons. As I listened I felt a vibrational current enter the top of my head and go through my body. This current traveled down through both hands and to the glass coffee mug I had in my hands. The cup shattered into tiny pieces. The contents were one-third full of a lukewarm latte. My favorite gray corduroy pants were drenched in light brown liquid. When I looked at my hands expecting to see blood, I was shocked to see there were no cuts on my hands. As I looked down at the mess, I remembered the Memorex commercial about how the sound was so good in the quality of the cassette tape it would break a wine glass in tiny pieces when the opera singer hit the high note. It was our first clue.

Cathy and I sat there stunned! What just happened? One of the owners of the coffee shop ran over and apologized profusely. He insisted on making me another latte. Of course, I accepted, after all, a gal cannot refuse a free latte. I am from Seattle. I laughed when I saw my replacement latte brought to me in a Styrofoam cup. The owner was not taking any chances! He had already lost one glass cup.

As Cathy and I tried to sort out what had happened, the discussion turned to the idea that this was a paranormal message. Cathy was sure it was some sort of message. I had no idea what it was. How to decipher it?

As it happened, a young man seated at the next table joined in our discussion. The universe being friendly provided us with some answers. He told us he had recently been studying paranormal abilities at John F. Kennedy University in San Francisco, California. Naturally I had never heard of the school but Cathy had. She said one of her sisters had done some research about schools with courses in the paranormal, and she had mentioned to Cathy this was an excellent program. The young man was pleased to hear she had heard of his school.

He proceeded to say that he was sure the glass breaking was some kind of paranormal sign and encouraged me to find a reputable psychic in the area. Now we were stuck. Cathy and I thought about who might know a psychic reader in the area. Cathy decided our South African friend Susan might. She did not, but told us another mutual friend, Ellen, would. Ellen was very helpful and directed me to Jean. She was a psychic and a teacher.

Jean gave me a psychic reading, my first. She said this event had not been random or just a coincidence. She felt it was a message to/for me. What was the significance of that date and time for me? I remembered that November 11th was originally Armistice Day after World War I. My grandmother had talked to me about President Wilson's goal of world peace and all nations communicating. At the time of this incident of the cup breaking I was working as a juvenile probation counselor, helping youth find other methods of solving differences without violence. The psychic did not think the date was as significant as the idea it was a holiday. I remember thinking she was not correct but I was confused. She was the psychic not me.

She also told me I was psychic. Now I wasn't sure if I believed her. I was surprised and skeptical. However, I did take some classes from her. We were taught about ESP, or intuition, clairvoyance, clairaudience, telluric, automatic writing, psychometry, and distant viewing. We learned about spirit guides, guardian angels, the thin veil that separates the living and the dead. To be aware and recognize there are evil forces in the paranormal world. Be skeptical and protect yourself with white light and a loving heart.

More pondering. Did I really want to do this? No, I was quite perplexed with the idea but I also trust the divine plan. I made a commitment to my spiritual path and have gone forward, sometimes kicking and screaming and often humbled or rather humiliated but moving in a different direction. Change is not easy for me but—-oh well! I continually have to get over myself. Change is not a secret. All of earth is change. Show me one tree that is the same year after year. The problem arose with my limited belief about life and choices. I still struggle. I think they call it the human experience.

I semi-embraced my new life. It was not easy going from a data-driven juvenile probation counselor to a "New Age" psychic who focuses on intuition and a knowing. Yet, it was not that hard either. If I could only remember to breathe. Breathing reads easier than it is.

The Healing Touch

In her second group of classes, Jean taught us how to direct and run the healing energy of love. She started by showing us how to run energy through our hands so each hand would send energy to the other hand. She asked us to notice if one hand was able to send stronger energy to the other hand. She asks us if we could feel the energy and asked us if we could see the energy. Well, I definitely felt the energy, it was a force and between my hands it felt like an invisible concertina and gave me more confidence.

We learned to direct the energy from our hands to an area on our own bodies. Could we feel that, yes or no? Next, we learned to direct the energy to another person. It was important prior to beginning this work to place yourself in God's protection and the loving light of white light. She was a religious person and used the term God; other people have used another word, such as the Creator, Source, or Divine Love to explain the spiritual nature of the activity. What is white light? The light that is depicted in paintings of the angels, the saints, and Jesus. It is intriguing to think how artists knew about the white/golden light auras of holy people. Did they really see it or was it just an artistic style tradition? Part of my education was learning that some people easily read auras or the light around people, and others don't. What a concept for a newbie to accept. Yet the artist's likeness of holy people usually included a golden or white aura. Wow, I guess this is some evidence to consider. These artists lived in different geographical areas, different time periods, and yet this similarity existed. Was I convinced people saw auras? No, but I have an open mind and discuss the topic with other people. Pretty interesting topic. First people explained to me that seeing an aura is not like seeing someone's eye or hair color. Rather it was more a light vapor quality. To begin we were asked to squint our eyes and focus on the head of an individual. It took me months to see anything and rarely do I see colors. Other people are much more gifted in this area and have seen things since they were children. I like that people who actually see energy fields can tell a lot about the person's life. My gift visually is secondary to what I am sensing, and what I see in my mind's eye, through my third eye in the center of my forehead. I find it fascinating that each person is different with their individual talents and ideally, we share our gifts for the whole of the common good. Go Us!

Following Guidance-Just Do It!

It has not been easy, but it could have been a lot worse if I did not listen to my inner guidance. Oh, and it did get worse. Like the time, I felt a "knowing" I was supposed to move but I did not want to move. A main line water pipe broke above my home. The house was located on a hill and the additional water flow caused the house to move, sliding slightly down the hill. The local government saw the problem, decided it was a hazard, and condemned the house. My son and I had to quickly find some place to stay. It was a scramble to find some place and really unnerving. Before we could move back into the house, it was burglarized and my passport was stolen. My son's prize fabric poster of the Doors was stolen too. We thought the neighbor kids did it but that was thin air thinking we had no proof except the kids were problematic and seemed smug after the burglary. As you know, smug behavior can feel disrespectful but it is not criminal. The point was not what we lost but rather what we gained. A new beginning in our lives. We both had to let go of our past and move into ourselves. It was a crossroad that I did not want to face, hence, the giant nudge from the universe. Now my image is one of being more open to following my path. However, my foot still sticks in the doorway sometimes and I need a push through the door. When this happens, I know I should have followed my intuition. It can be as small of a deal as knowing I should put my charger in my purse, only to discount the knowing because my phone's battery is 100%. Then, there I am, finding out that someone else needed a charger or needing it myself because I was gone much longer than I planned. Oh, well, next time, and yes, I have concluded there always seems to be a next time. Part of my work is to remind people how much they already know. Part of my work is to help people sort out some of their confusion about their life. Part of my work is to remind myself to follow my intuition. It is always a cocreative process of the individual, me, and the sacred oneness of God/Source.

Cultural Reality Blocks Talents

I would like to think this is a common behavior but I am not sure. I look at the amazing Olympic athletes and their drive, talent and perseverance to succeed. Can they really be blocking their talent? They are amazing in their performance! Right!?

Here is how I know I block my abilities. I mention in this book about the bruise disappearing on a face. Here are a few others examples. I decided to call my friend Sam and have a friendly chat. We have been friends since high school. I dialed, this was in the old days of dialing phones and not pressing buttons, and he immediately answered. He said he knew it was me because this particular phone was not connected to the phone line. It was in the same room as he was reading a book. So, it was an easy pick-up.

I was stunned because who does that. Phones are supposed to be attached to a phone line. We talked, had a nice chat and hung up. Of course, my mind was wondering, much more than Sam's attitude of "I knew it was you." A few weeks later I called another friend or a client. Now, I do not remember. What I do know is they were so grateful that I was able to get through on the phone line. The line had been dead for days. We talked and I made the mistake of telling her that the phone line might not be fixed. I seemed to have this ability to call people when the phone is not working. This information startled her. She felt it was not possible. The line crackled and was dead again. I tried to call her back but the line was not working. I never called someone again unless their phone was working. Another example was a key. I was living in a condo and had a roommate. We had a storage area in the basement. I never had any problem with opening our unit. Weeks if not months went by. She asked to borrow my key once and went down to open the storage. The storage lock did not open. When she came back upstairs from the basement she checked her keys with my key. The key I had been using was not the storage locker key. I was never able to use that key again for my storage area. I knew now it would not work.

I think I have mentioned I do not see vibrational beings from different dimension, such as spirits, trolls or angels, except in my third eye. At one time, I could but again I found it too distracting and prayed to have the ability removed. The distraction was night driving downtown in Seattle, and seeing a black panther running along my auto and eventually sprinting in front of my car, I hitting my brake, and the big cat disappearing in the darkness. I freaked out with drama of *what if's*.

On occasion, I still do see visions. Once, I saw Kwan Yin, in my office area. Kwan Yin is the Asian goddess of compassion and mercy. Kwan Yin has been a part of my experience since 1970. I bought two statues of her likeness when my son was an infant. One is Chinese and one is possibly Thai or Burmese. One of the practitioners had been working with Kwan Yin energy, and I saw the goddess not the practitioner when she walked by me. When I told her what I had seen, she affirmed that was quite possible because she was working with Kwan Yin. My goal in sharing this information is to remind people even if we limit ourselves we still have plenty to offer each other.

AH HA Moments: Breathe AH-HA

Fear helps me acknowledge my limiting beliefs and allows me to become aware of the focus of my pain. Even if my fear blocks some of my talent, my soul knows the way. Trusting with loving kindness of being enough and I know joy follows.

Spirit Guides

What is a Spirit Guide?

What are spirit guides? You might ask. A spirit guide is someone who can guide you in your intuitive world. How do people find out who their spirit guides are? The way I first found mine was meditating and asking for my spirit guides to come forth. This is also a way to call upon my animal totems to be seen.

What is an Animal Totem?

An animal totem is a creature that has characteristics a person needs to learn and will be helpful to your spiritual and emotional development. Animal totems can change through one's lifetime. Yes, you can have more than one animal totem.

It helps to pay attention to coincidences regarding creatures. For example, the frog totem has come into my life to help with my next stage of life path. I received lots of frog messages in a dream and the next day I received a gift of a picture puzzle of different frogs. Years ago, someone gave me a pottery lidded pot with a frog handle. I felt drawn to place it outside my front door as a welcoming message. Only now do I feel the need to truly study the habits of the frog to help me better understand myself and be of service. Most recently, a frog was included in my vision board. Sometimes, you really do not have to put that much thinking effort into the question, rather your effort is to be alert to any signs in your surroundings.

Spirit Guides/Totem Animals Test

How can you know for sure your guidance is good and not evil? How can you be sure that you are not being misled by evil? Many people have asked me that. My answer is through prayer and meditation. This action keeps my vibration in the pink. Here is a tried and true method. While you are in meditation and see your guides, throw a ball of white light to them. If they catch it, they are in the light. If they do not catch it or dodge it, they are evil. Find the ones with your best and higher intention and move forward. I once knew someone who believed they channeled a well-known spiritual figure. Once they did some energy work on me. I felt vulnerable and put an energy shield around me. I saw in my mind's-eye that it was indeed the spiritual figure. However, upon closer observation I saw the channeled guide was holding a mask in front of her face and was not the acclaimed spiritual person. I do not know if the person channeling the entity knew or not. I tried to talk to them about it but the conversation was shut down immediately.

AH HA Moments

I was not my idea of someone who *should* have this amount of energetic talent/ability. For instance, I have a temper, can be grumpy and self-critical. Sometimes I blurt words that might be true without my opinion being asked. No one that knows me says that I am not opinionated. I am. At the same time, as I age, my opinions allow for me to recognize my ideas are my personal experiences with my baseline as ego centered awareness. It allows me to understand what the saying "Walk a mile in my shoes" means. It means we all have a different pair of shoes and the feet that goes with them.

Yes, I have the reputation of being gentle and kind but is that enough? I am also a good listener and really care about people's feelings and life experiences. At the same time, I do believe in living life on life's terms. My clarity is the fire of truth. Fire is cleansing, think of the Phoenix rising from the ashes. I have risen from the ashes more than once.

Am I enough? The answer to this question comes from self-acceptance and embracing self-love. Self-love is the most important lesson I have learned in this journey. The saying, "Love your neighbor as yourself" is only doable if we are able to love to our inner core of our living essence.

Energetic Basics

What are Downloads?

Downloads are just that; an energy vibration comes through your crown chakra and you can feel it. Different downloads feel differently. The first download was most likely, the first time I experienced the energetic vibration on November 11th. This experience was new and thus it was quite something to me. Most recently, I was visiting a friend. I had had a very good day of being hydrated, meditated, exercised and relaxed. I walked into my room and plugged my computer and phone into the wall for charging. I stepped back and was near the bedpost. Immediately, I felt this huge pressure coming into my body; it was a grounding force. The energy was so forceful I felt my knees buckle, and felt this immense pressure on my shoulders and head. Placing my hand on the bed for support I walked towards the rocking chair and plopped down. I waited a few seconds and wondered if I could get up. I tried to get up but the amount of energy I needed to get up was more than I had. I waited a few minutes and the download was completed, and I was able to easily get up, and continue on with my daily activity. Later my friend and I were talking. I realized that unlike previous downloads that have left me trying to reconnect with myself and my environment this was not like that. The way I explained is if you had been on a boat, and have developed sea legs, when you return to dry land it takes a bit for your body to reconnect with non-moving ground. In this case, my body felt pushed down towards the earth.

Each download has its own characteristics. Some of the downloads remind me of fairy dust that I have seen in pictures in children's books. It is light, and feels like sparkly drops of happiness touching my body; my body joyfully feeling the effects and welcoming the sensation through my head and skin. This type of download rarely requires a person to sit. A person can enjoy the sensation and continue about their daily routine, as a walk in a gentle rain.

Another type of download is an intermittent download. This download is more intense and feels like a bolt of something has entered your field of energy. This bolt has come suddenly and my legs have gotten wobbly and I feel stunned. Another bolt comes through, and possibly a third or fourth. None as strong as the first bolt, nevertheless the effect is noticeable. Once, while I was experiencing this my ability to speak was compromised and I had to wait for the download to finish the energy transfer. During this type of download my proprioception is way off and I feel very clumsy in my body. I might even trip. Again, this passes fairly quickly and my normal gait returns.

During all of these downloads my energy field has undergone a significant shift. I am not sure what the longest download is. I do know sometimes after the download if I am home I need a lot of time to sit quietly and blend my old energy with the new. I do a lot of breath exercises to stay in sensation in my body.

Someone asked me if I have ever felt this in a dangerous place, such as driving on the freeway. The answer is no. I am always in a safe environment. The universe is gentle with me and I appreciate it. It is rare that a lot of human emotion comes with the download, rather it feels like an energetic tweak. After the transmute, I felt some melancholy sadness. It was there and in three seconds it was gone. My feelings returned to a homeostatic familiar DNA pattern. Just for comparison, the earth's clearing of heavy energy is different because it does not feel like I need to integrate this into my being. It has a boundary and is a separate action.

White Light Protects

Part of our training with Jean was putting yourself in the protection of white light. She talked about envisioning yourself surrounded by white light. This would protect you. I had a little training, very little (white belt), in karate. I did understand the concept of throwing energy with a focus. One day I was walking our dog Kasey. He was a black and white springer spaniel. He was on leash and we were strolling through the neighborhood. All of a sudden, a Pitbull started to run across the street towards Kasey.

Both of us just stood there and stared. The Pitbull began to leap, jaws open heading towards Kasey's throat. I threw white light energy around Kasey, my first instinct to protect him. The Pitbull now had all four feet off the ground and was inches from Kasey's throat. The Pitbull hit an invisible shield, and his jaw and head smacked up against it and he bounced off. Stunned, the Pitbull looked startled, as if to say, "What just happened?" and turned and ran off. It was the first time I had witnessed the miracle of white light. Neither Kasey or I were hurt but we turned around and immediately went home. We had more than enough adventure for the day.

Another story I enjoy telling is the time I was downtown. It was a wet and dark night. The streets were slippery. The crosswalk light signaled Walk so I began to cross the street. I was in a hurry to catch the bus across the street. My focus was on catching the bus. As I stepped off the curb I heard people gasping. I immediately looked to my left and saw a city bus racing through a red light. More gasps. I shout something like "Not on my watch" or "Not going to happen" and put my left arm straight out with the hand bent and held upright, the signal to stop the bus. The bus stopped. People were telling me how lucky I was that the bus was able to stop. Difficult because it was accelerating to go through the stoplight. I did not explain what I did and felt pretty comfortable no one noticed what I did. However, this man, dressed in a brown trench coat, looking very mainstream, said, "Nice catch!" and smiled. I was a bit startled to be seen, smiled back, waved and ran to catch my bus. My adrenal glands were working overtime. Wow, what just happened, I was almost hurt or killed. Did that guy really see me throw energy or was it just a comradely kind of remark? I was pretty sure he did see it. My assumption was based on his knowing look as to what just happened, that he read energy. I was grateful for the training and the ability to protect myself, but also said to myself to look before I begin to cross the street. Also, reminded myself the only times I have been close to being hit by a vehicle was in a crosswalk.

Only a couple of other times have people commented on this ability to throw energy. Once I was in the Stockholm airport with a group of massage therapists travelling together. I was one of their tour guides. A small group of men, very drunk, came up to some of the female massage therapists. Two were particularly obnoxious, refused to leave and were very pushy, trying to engage them in conversation. It was obvious the women were uncomfortable. I did not consciously plan this, but I was feeling protective and annoyed for them. Slowly the men began to back off and they finally left. Two of the massage therapists came up to me after the incident. Both said they read energy, and told me they saw me push the men energetically away from the group. I was surprised. I did not know I did it. I knew my feelings were protective, and certainly my intent was that they leave. Intention is everything. Another time I was ushering at the Northwest Asian Theater. Someone was annoying. In this case, I think I was the one target. The other usher at the door read energy and told me that she saw me push that person away energetically. At first I did not believe I had the ability to do that, so she explained she saw me push my energy field toward his solar plexus with a gentle nudge or push. He did back away and leave. This is always very appealing to me, when others can see energetic fields expand and contract. I rarely see. I sense things. It is just easier for me as I am a visual person. I am sure being a visually energetic seer would not be helpful for me to stay engaged in life; much too distracting.

Rosary Story in St. Joseph Church

People have asked me if I know for certain if my work is good and not evil driven. The simple answer is love. I do not doubt I work in the light ever since I began my work thirty years ago. My doubt was centered on "Why me?" Surely there is someone better suited temperamentally for this task. I have the emotions of an artist and naturally am reactive to my environment. It seemed to me that a person that has a mellow and a centered outlook is a better choice. My ideal candidate was not me. This prejudice towards myself, was a huge burden to my soulful outlook, and

I went to St. Joseph's Church in Seattle to pray about it. I was praying and feeling inadequate for the task that loomed before me. Also, I was skeptical: was this not my own ego-driven mind, not from a sacred place of love. This church was almost empty, there were just a few people there. It had this feeling of coziness, not all the lights were lit, and shadows played along part of the walls. As I prayed I looked down and found a rosary on the pew. The rosary was crystal cut beads and had a medal of St. Anne on it. Somewhere on the rosary it said 1951, the year I was born.

I thought, "Wow, is this rosary for me?" I did not want to steal it. Especially in a church, that seemed horrible. Maybe I could take it to the rectory's Lost and Found. Maybe I should just leave it there. As I was pondering a man approached me. He had been a couple rows behind me. My initial response was fear. People usually do not approach strangers in church especially men to women. He had a strong lithe body and had the tattoos of someone who practiced Charismatic Catholicism. I believe he was Filipino but now I do not remember for sure. I had read about Filipino faith healers and knew one person that had gone to one for her illness and felt like their abilities cured her. I am telling you this because if Spirit was going to send me anyone to verify my work a Filipino man was a good choice. He started talking to me, he had the blue cross markings on his forehead. He spoke with fervor and conviction. He raised one arm with his elbow slightly bent and pointed upwards Yes, he said, that rosary is for you. He said some other things and went back to his pew. I do not remember what else he said. I was a bit in surprise. MMM, I would like to say I completely embraced him, but he scared me. He seemed a little nutty to me, a bit too over the top religious for my comfort. Nothing wrong with his religious fervor, it was just that I had not seen anything like that except on television. People in my world usually do not approach strangers in church and the charismatic man telling me it was my rosary was even more unusual. What was really amazing was that it had the St. Anne medal on the side and the crucifix said 1951, the same year I was born. How was that possible?

I prayed regularly with that rosary. It was a great comfort. One day I realized the rosary was gone. Did I drop it? Did it just vanish in thin air? Considering how I received it I could not rule out anything. I never did find it. My theory is that the time for that particular rosary was done. Over the years, I have used different rosaries including an Irish Celtic ring rosary that one of my aunts gave me. The rosary is my choice of a prayer tool only because I grew up with it and am very comfortable with the formal meditative/prayer method. My method is right for me and I encourage you to find you own method of prayer, reflection and meditation.

Angel People

What are angel people? Well, as far as I know I made up the term, but you can google it. Angel people by my experience are human beings who have special abilities. There was a wave of light workers that came to Earth. They seemed to have human and angel DNA. I first encountered an angel person in 1989. I was doing energetic clearing on people. I noticed that some clients had this tar-like substance stuck on their back, a lot of it. So, I dug it out, and put the tar into a ball and stuffed it into a bag of protective white light. As I continue to dig, I realized that this person had some sort of energetic wings attached to their back. I continued to clean them. The wings reminded me of the angel's wings from the Renaissance era painting. They were large, thick and luxurious. I do not remember if I told the first person about the angel wings. If someone had told me my back had angel's wings, I would have questioned it big time. More clients' appointments centered around a session to have their angel wings cleaned and unstuck. The second client, we did discuss it and talked about what it meant. Most people have an intuitive knowing about themselves and it is wise to listen and learn from the client; the cocreative process. I believe in the cocreative process of energetic work.

We are all different. I had a knowing these people were here to help with the transformation of the earth's vibration. They came here with the angel lightness knowledge but can become confused by people's behavior. This confusion causes pain, hurt emotions and feelings of mistrust. They forgot their mission for the earth and with confusion became fearful and sometimes angry. Later, when I become a massage therapist/energy worker, I still met clients with this energetic situation on their back. People were grateful for the knowledge. They smiled when I was able to cocreate with them and encourage them to shine brightly. People have asked me if I am an angel person and I never think that. Rather, I was the facilitator to remind the Angel people who they are and the real purpose on the earth. The song *Calling All Angels* by Jane Siberry had just come out and it was reawakening people to their gentle angelic vibration. It was released years later by another group. It felt to me that it was signaling another group of people to remember their light.

One time a client wanted a friend, maybe their sister, to be in the room during the session. She had the angel people wings. Next time I saw them both, the friend had no memory of the session. This happened twice. My guess is only the people with the angelic vibrational field had the capacity to remember these conversations. This reassured me that even if lots of people were around, only the people who were the recipients of the message would hear it and remember it. If people are speaking a language to a friend, and you do not speak the language, most likely you will not be able to remember what you heard. Same idea.

Hidden Spirits Rest in/on the Body

Sometime other entities rest on a body. Once I found a gargoyle deeply hidden on a person's body. I had no idea that gargoyles were real. I thought they were figments of a medieval artist's mind. Here is the story. I began to pull a dark energy form, a tarlike substance, from the back of the client's body. It appears more and more as some sort of entity. It had been compressed and compacted into her energy field. As the energy was pulled it had more room to expand, and expand it did. As I released the entity from her back and put it in a pink bag of love for disposal, I marveled at the discovery that a creature, like one we see on a medieval building, can really exist. I have also seen an energetic furry animal. These types take energy from a person and do not help them live fuller lives.

Removing Curses

Yes, I have removed curses. Most of the curses have been passed down in families. Two families are feuding and one person curses the other. Energetically to me I see an image of a black lone thread, rather like spider legs. The curse reaches out from the distant past, decades go by and still this spider leg intermingles with the descendants of the cursed person. The curse flows into their DNA, and yet it is really more thought essence than a mark on their soul. Marks on the soul are through your own actions, not someone else's behavior including ancestors. By following the spindly leg back to its origins, a picture emerges of the original insult and curse. As you can guess, the energy at that moment in time is full of anger and hate. Their intention is fully focused to do as much harm as possible. Higher vibration energy can dissipate the heavier vibration by engulfing the scene and people with love. The black line can be dissolved or sent to a black hole. As it dissolves, one can to follow it back to the present time. Fill the empty space with the infinite love of the universe.

Most recently a curse removal involved the Chicago Cubs. The Chicago Cubs had not won the World Series since 1906. A legend developed that says the team and organization was cursed by a disgruntled goat owner. I know a goat owner, and this is a very believable story. This curse stopped the baseball team from ever winning the World Series again. It looked like the Cubs were on their way to losing the series, yet again. The Cleveland Indians had a 3-1 lead over the Chicago Cubs. The next game would be the last one if the Cubs lost again. More talk about the curse; I wondered, was there really a curse? Intrigued, and wanting the Cubs to have an equal playing field, I decided to do some psychic investigating. Through my third eye vision I focused on the team, the possible curse, and to see its effect. Yes, there was a curse. Interestingly, the curse was more about the space where the ball field was located.

The field is the oldest original location for a ball field in the United States. I wonder if the entire curse would have been broken if they had moved the baseball field location? It was a powerful curse! The energy rose high above and around the stadium and hung like an angel of soot mixed with vapor, giving it a grayish tone. Not exactly the most pleasant place to work. I wondered if people in the administration office had problems with depression that lifted when the curse was lifted. Of course, winning a world series could also uplift mood.

AH HA Moments

The false sense of who we are and why it matters. It matters because being a stranger to ourselves is lonely and not aloneness. When we do not know ourselves how can we truly entertain ourselves? For example, a person wakes up at four in the morning. The person can feel the stillness of the night and feel lonely. No one to converse with, the street is empty of noise, and you are alone with yourself and your thoughts. On the other hand, what if a person wakes up at four in the morning, revels in the stillness, and loves the aloneness as a way to be separate, yet connected with the energy of the universe. For some it is their most creative time.

Supernatural Painting

Guardian Angel Story
Photo of painting is available on website.

My phone began ringing in the middle of the night. Half-asleep I picked up the phone. It was a voice I had never heard. He identified himself and began to speak. He informed me that my son had been in a car accident and he was now at Tacoma General Hospital in the emergency room. He made sure that I knew this was not an April Fool's joke. The serious tone in his voice already convinced me that this call was legitimate. He told me that my son had facial lacerations but no broken bones. Thank God, I thought. Should I call someone to go with me? Well, it was in the middle of the night and I did not want to disturb anyone. First mistake. Lesson learned, remember friends like to be there for you. I begin the drive from Seattle to Tacoma. As I am driving I go over the words the caller had said. Facial lacerations, what does that mean? I should have asked how many, how deep, but I just wanted to go to Tacoma and be with my son. I arrived at Tacoma General and another mother and her brother were there. They had driven down from Green Lake. Her son had been driving a used New York checker taxi, which belonged to the uncle. The teens used the wheels to get to our family beach house. My son had invited a few male friends to go fishing that weekend or so I thought. Really it was a teen party and some of his high school female friends were also invited. The girls, newly arrived, had wanted some ketchup and mustard for their hot dogs and buns. My son and the driver offered to go to the store to buy these items. They jumped in the car and went along the country road to the store. On their return home, the car crashed, after going high in the air, wrapping around a power pole, and landing hard on the ground. The electric power in the area was now gone because of the crash. It was a really bad crash. The attending sheriff's deputy was so upset he took the next two days off work. The seatbelt broke upon impact. The engine unbolted and flew 14 feet hitting a tree. They were both safe with minor injuries, luckily both kids were wearing seatbelts. It changed our life.

That night I had been painting watercolors. It is not unusual for me to paint on the weekends. Mostly I do abstract types of art and sometime figures. This time I painted two figures, one of someone who resembled my son and the other an unknown figure standing in front of him. The figure of my son had a red patch on his chest area. He was released from the hospital that night and we drove home and talked. My son was interested in seeing the picture so I showed it to him. We both agreed there was a resemblance. I told him I was not sure who the figure in front of him was and wondered if it was me. He said, "No Mom, it is my guardian angel." He told me the person in the picture had been at the accident. He explained she seemed to come out of nowhere on this empty country road. She talked to him and told him he would be okay. As my son saw the police car lights speeding toward the accident she disappeared. He never did see how she came or went but assumed she came through the woods. After the accident, my son began to value his life, his time, and felt lucky he had a future and did not want to waste it. In short, he started doing his homework and being physically active again. We had turned the corner. It gave me a sense of peace to know my son's guardian angel was there protecting him from serious harm and I had a picture to prove it.

The Flower Painting

Have a photo of this but it is a reshoot of a copy of a photo, quality not great.

One day I was painting a watercolor and decided to show it to my psychic teacher. It was a picture of pinkish tulips and a balloon. When I entered her home to my surprise she had a basket of pink tulips and a balloon. The colors were the same. It was enough for me to believe I was more psychic than I gave myself credit for. Even I had no logical reason for this coincidence. The other students thought it was cool. If it had just been the tulips… but tulips, the colors and the balloon. I was becoming more of a believer of this phenomenon. I was still a newbie and did not know exactly where all this psychic behavior would lead. It did not matter because it was a path that seemed to be SHOUTING at me and I chose to follow all that drama and attention. Pretty hard to ignore it. I wonder sometimes what would have happened if I had chosen to ignore it. MMM, based on the times I did not and suffered the consequences, most likely I would have died with the expectation to complete my spiritual assignment without my body. This is way more fun, most of the time.

Spirit Art Pictures

A few spirit pictures are on website.

Today a friend was telling our book group about such a coincidence. Her family dog, Fancy had recently died. She had had the dog for many years and she was missing her pal. The dog died comfortably, at home, and a hospice caretaker helped with the final moments. The best part was that in her son's room, a stone sculpture, of low relief over his bed hangs on the wall over his bed. After Fancy's death, he went into his bedroom he saw an image of Fancy in the low relief stone sculpture. He called his mother into his room and asked her if she noticed anything about it. She immediately saw the resemblance to Fancy, too. How was it that no one had ever noticed that? It had been there for years. It jogged my mind of a memory. Years ago, I painted watercolor pictures and much to my surprise, some of the paintings periodically changed. It reminded me of the book, *The Picture of Dorian Gray*, only in this case, my paintings were more abstract and obscure. Still the colors changed and so did some of the images. Some of the pictures felt like if it was a high-five from the universe or spirit people; an encouragement to keep going and learn more about this paranormal world. I was still in my skeptical stage of "Is this real?" I was not the only one who noticed the changes in the pictures. Weird, was a comment I heard now and again. And guess what? The spirit art pictures stopped changing. I have not thought about this art process for years. It served its purpose, and was no longer a communication tool for the spirits. Along the same lines, a palm reader once read my hand palm. The next week she read my palm again and said, "This is strange. Your palm has changed. Nobody's palm hand lines changes in a week!" Or do they? This might have happened to you or someone you know. Is it possible we have a lot more choice in our destiny then we give ourselves credit for?

AH HA Moments

Painting is my comfort. Sometimes as I paint, I think about life.

The process of life, once I let go, felt like a spool of ribbon dropped with a force of its own unraveling and opening. Luckily and with gratitude, I have met other spools sometimes racing, sometimes rolling slowly, sometimes quiet like a summer day laying on the earth, watching the moving clouds. With luck, you have a friend who enjoys the quiet moments of nature. Talking and sharing your experiences in my life has helped with the loneliness of change. Sometimes, much like when we go through the birth channel in single fashion to be born, we travel singularly to reach our new destination. On the other hand, change is normal, stagnant living is not.

Psychic Line

I became involved with the psychic phone line through another psychic friend. Not sure how I met these people. The year was around 1993. There was not much interfacing on the computer, just the phone and most people had landlines. My memory is very vague, but I think it was through a friend-of-a-friend sort of connection. One of these gals had been approached to work on the psychic line, and they were recruiting psychics. I have forgotten her name or where she was—somewhere in New England—she encouraged me to apply. To apply you were required to do one or two readings on different people. If they felt your information was accurate you were hired. I believe another requirement was a cassette recording of a reading but I never did that. The phone reading was all that was needed; plus, an independent phone line available for psychic line clients.

Stories

1. "What happened to my brother?" seems like an innocent question. Right? It was not! It was

a test and she knew what happened to him. So, I raised my vibration and tuned into the energy. I felt all his pain. He had been brutally murdered. As I remember, he had been grabbed from behind and repeatedly stabbed. He did not want to die and his realization of his potential death left him screaming in fear, angry and beyond rage. This was not how he thought his life would end. I believe he also knew the attacker and felt betrayed. The physical pain was also unbearable. Honestly, I do not remember if I was able to clear his path to go to a higher vibration. The lesson for me was to protect myself and my own energy field. Feeling all his pain both emotionally and physically was horrible. I remember it to this day and it is a great reminder to be cautious and to put yourself in the protection of white light or golden light of love. When I spoke to the caller about her brother's death, she affirmed that yes, he had died a violent death. She was almost matter of fact. At the time, I thought it was cold-hearted of her not to warn me, and maybe she did not realize the consequences of her request. She did not seem upset with my horrible experience. However, now I know that personal traumas can create an unawareness of another's personal safety. After the phone call ended I disconnected from the psychic line and cleared my energy field as best as I could. As I write this now, it occurs to me it was really wonderful that she called. The two siblings connected and both had a little more peace in being able to communicate with each other. Once his pain was cleared, he could let his sister know he was ready to move forward in his soul's life. She was able to share his experience of receiving his own grace through love, to move forward towards the light.

2. The businessman from London. One of my biggest surprises was realizing I could understand business matters. No, really! Here is the story. A businessman called and wanted

my assessments about the personalities he dealt with in his business negotiations. He asked me to assess situations and discuss the different personalities. He also might have asked me about different financial ventures. He wanted a winning edge to his business activities. We were both surprised at my awareness and success. I think he called maybe three times. As I realized I had this ability, I started wondering about the ethics of doing this, and whether it violated people's personal space and boundaries. I was not reading their energy in their body, rather I was reading their thoughts hovering around their body. Reading their energy without their permission is definitely a boundary violation, but reading the thoughts hovering around the body is a gray area and a good topic for an ethics discussion.

3. A common theme people telephoned about was lost objects. This is not an area where I have lots of talent. This only works for me if I

can follow the energy trail of the lost object. Sometimes, if I call out the lost object, the energy path directs me to a brighter spot. It almost calls to me or waves hello, "Here I am, over here!" It is more difficult on the phone, with no pictures; I had to use my mind's eye to guide me to possibilities. I remember one time I saw an attic with an entry on the ceiling. There was in fact an attic with this type of entrance in the caller's house. Then she hung up the phone to get a ladder and check if her lost object was there. People were restricted by phone cords and landlines. Plus, it cost them so much a minute. They could always call back and talk to someone else if their lost object was not found. As I remember, different psychic readers listed their areas of expertise for a caller to receive the exact type of help they sought.

Working the Psychic Line

Working the psychic line, my goal was to help people with their lives and to gain confidence in myself through practicing my abilities. It seemed like a sweet deal. All I needed to do was install a separate line, sign on when I wanted to work, and wait for the calls. I talked to many different people, mostly in the United States, occasionally Canada and once in England. It was much harder than it looked. The most noteworthy situation was what happened as the calls progressed. Often the first call was full of light and love, the next call not quite as light, until each call became progressively darker in the energy...

Once I had a call from a young woman from the Midwest area, I think from Canada. Her energy field was clear and her chakras were balanced. She started talking about her childhood, and said she had an ideal childhood, and had no major traumas in her life. It was awe inspiring for me to know people can live without trauma but still have natural tragic experiences. Tragedy and trauma are different.

AH HA Moments

Tragedy is the outward appearance of an occurrence, such as a young mother dying and not being able to see her children grow to adulthood.

Trauma is the process of inward thoughts and feelings about an occurrence, such as a repeated memory of your mother dying in pain when you were a child.

Body Awareness

Chakra Balancing

It was during my work on the psychic line that I realized how shut down some of the women were in connecting to the earth. Maybe men too, but many of the women calling the psychic line considered themselves New Age evolved souls, and believed that denying their human impulses and their earthly connection was more pleasing to God/spiritual essence. They believed human feeling negates spirituality. As I read their energy, I was surprised how bright and strong the heart, throat, forehead and the top of the head chakras were. The lower chakras of the root, sacrum, and the solar plexus were sluggish or closed. Visually in my third eye, this seemed to create a feeling that they were out of their body and not grounded. Many felt they had reached a higher understanding of the evolution of a human being. Not sure, sometimes I did not feel the same way, but it was not constant. People comment on my earthy grounded energy. As more of us pursue our sacred paths, we began to understand the importance of getting ALL the chakras balanced through chakra meditation, yoga, and gardening and other activities. Just doing it will push you along the path of balanced enlightenment. In my experience, human beings evolve much faster if they connect with all their chakras. Each one has a purpose. Now, let me put in a plug for a chakra balancing meditation once a week. Ideally, it takes place in a quiet room. A guided meditation through the chakras is wonderful. But even sitting or standing on a commuter bus you can go through a mindful meditation process with the body. Once done, a quick connection with the chakra keeps a person mindful of their chakras. For me, particularly, I have a propensity to dwell in my head with lots of thoughts. So, for people like me, it is important to really center yourself in your root/sacrum area/tailbone area and put your breath there. The root chakra is the color red so red underpants or visualizing red in this area is also very helpful. At the time while I knew balanced chakras were very important, I did not think it was a problem for me. My chakras were tuned to perfection. Three fingers back and one forward was a clue but I missed it. Rather, I decided I was more spiritually advanced than that. But in fact, when other people's behavior bothers me I need to look in the mirror. Of course, regular reflection of personal interactions helps too. If someone's behavior bothers me, I ask myself, why am I bothered and what is my part in this? Often, this exercise results in clarity of action and thought. If my actions are clean with integrity of purpose, then my chakras have a better chance of staying balanced.

The human experience creates a physical network of love for each person. We are of service to others when we serve in the Grace of the action of love. The chakra creates an ability to stay connected with the human experience and the earth and the light energy of the sky. Does God/Source have chakras? Most likely not. Chakras are a physical aspect of the human experience. It is part of our sensory experience to understand the physical connectedness of living in a body. Do animals have chakras? I do not know. It is an interesting idea to consider. Certainly, trees and rocks have telepathic abilities, but they really have no need to be earthier. They are earthy and trees have a magnificent connection with each other through their root structures and an uncanny ability to communicate with each other telepathically. I have communicated with the same species of trees in one geographical area, only to have the same tree species, someplace else, let me know they know who I am. When I asked how that was possible, they explained through telepathic thoughts because the trees near my home had told them about me. Kind of cool, huh?

Walking with the Earth

By chance, I went to a healing ceremony at a New Age Book Store led by a Native American Shaman. I decided to work with Native American elders and medicine people to begin to understand a fuller concept of connecting with the earth. I noticed that many if not all Native Americans walk in a very grounded earthy fashion. I saw most Caucasians walking almost on air. Just last year I realized that native people walk *with* the earth, while I was taught as a child we walk *on* the earth. Intention is an important factor in our reality. It appears to affect us in many ways that we have not always considered. I have learned to walk and dance with my feet connected to the earth. Once I was at a sacred native circle. It included dancing. Thomas, a member of one of the local Native American tribes, complimented me on my dancing and told me that I KNEW how to dance. I smiled and thought, mmm, I know how to dance, and have been given compliments in the past for my moves. He was talking about something else, my dancing body's deep connection with the earth/sky. It took me a minute to understand what he actually meant. He repeated it to make sure I understood. It was such a compliment for me to hear. I cherish the memory. A few years later he died at a relatively young age, early forties.

Self-Care

Another aspect of being available for intuitive energetic work is self-care. When I worked the psychic line, my plan was to work for a period of two hours at a time. My own comfort was a must to do the best reading for callers. So, before I signed on to the line, I would get comfortable on my futon sofa with a soft blanket and pillows. I had extra water and a cup of tea. I signed on to the general switchboard. The calls began. The first call was usually an amazing dazzle. The caller had a high vibration energy and it was an easy joyful call. As the calls progressed the energy of the callers became heavier and heavier with their stories and their intent. Finally, their intent was not to obtain information, rather the call was an obscene sexual call or the person was angry, possibly drunk. Why did this happen? It became apparent to me that each call, unless it was completely cleared of the caller's energy, mingled with the psychic's (me) and my vibration field became denser, and a slightly lower vibration. Think of a rain cloud; as the rain cloud grows it attracts more water moisture to it, and it becomes denser, darker and full of water. Water in Asian culture signifies emotions. In this case, the emotions from the callers became attached to the reader's energy field and absorbed the denser emotional vibrations of fear and anger. Go into a room filled with angry people and the tension is so thick you can cut it with a knife. The body often will become tense. Go into a room filled with love and joyous people and a smile spreads across your own face.

Sometimes the body is a lot smarter than we give it credit for being aware. I sometimes watch my body language. Even if I have told my brain this is okay and a necessary interaction, my body will disagree. I might step back, fold my arms, move away from the interactions, and cause my stomach to tighten. So even if I do not get it, my body does, and is my friend. I am sure all of us have noticed this in ourselves. Children often are still very much in their body awareness and can be very reliable in what they are sensing in their surroundings.

What is an easy fix to clear the energy? Putting your feet in a tub of Epsom salts helps greatly. It does not have to be hot water, nicely warm works just as well, maybe even better. Soak your feet for twenty minutes or so. Another trick is to zip up your energy field prior to beginning the work. The back zipper goes from the tail bone, up the spine, up over the head, to just under the lip. In the front of the body the zip line is in the center from the pubic bone to the right below the lower lip of the mouth. Also, another self-care tip is to rest. Energy work requires more protein and more rest. It is physically demanding work. A sports nutritionist who understood energy work once compared it to running a marathon. I do not know if that is completely true, but her point was made. I eat more protein and encourage other energy workers to do the same. It does not have to be animal protein. Any exercise that uses your legs and arms you are empowering the lymph system to do its job of moving toxins from the body to be discharged. Walking is another great way to clear energy. Walking is also a great way to meditate with your body's motion. Also, drink plenty of water to flush your system of toxins. It is not unusual when you do a lot of energy work to want the quick energy of sugar. If you know you are doing lots of energy work, eating a small amount of sugar or carb is helpful. It provides a light boost for quick energy. It is not a substitute for a well-balanced meal.

I say this, knowing I sometimes forget to eat dinner until 8:30 PM.

Caution, super-caution, burnt-out happens with energy workers too. Be mindful of the number of clients you see and the self-care. I am adding this because I just had a conversation with a friend of mine. She has heard that some practitioners lose their abilities because they are drawing from a past life experience and their practice is not rooted in the be present now stage. I also think some practitioners do not treat themselves like a precious object. Know yourself in this life and accept superheroes are in the movies not in your home. Most twelve steps group use the acronym HALT and caution against being too **H**ungry, **A**ngry, **L**onely or **T**ired. It really is good advice for most of us.

AH HA Moments

Self-care begins with paying attention to your breath. Listen now to your breathing. It might be a comfort.

Mexico Connections

Visitors from Mexico: Counselors

One summer, Sonia and Maria, two Mayan astrologers from Mexico, came to Seattle to lecture about the Mayan calendar. A friend of theirs, Carol, had urged them to come to Seattle. She took care of all the arrangements, found venues for their talks, and offered her home to them for a place to stay. Two of them were cigarette smokers. This information is important later. I read the East-West Bookstore's quarterly bulletin about this talk. Sonia was a counselor, and an expert on the Family Constellation System. Maria was trained as an architect, and used sacred geometry in her readings and her paintings. Both had been trained with some knowledge of the Mayan Calendar. The lecture was very interesting and informative. After the lecture, when the crowd had left, I walked outside, and I saw one of the lecturers smoking. We began to talk and we had an instant connection. I introduced myself and told them about my energetic work. Carol suggested we all connect at her home. It was very generous of her. It was decided that Sonia and I would trade services to experience each other's talents.

After I arrived Maria also wanted to experience a treatment. As life happens Maria did receive a treatment. She went to get some items from the SUV. The car's hatchback door was open and she hit her head on its edge. By this time, I had had some training in Reiki and also used my healing touch training. I immediately began sending healing light to her forehead. A bump was forming on her head and the skin was starting to discolor. I looked up, no one else had seen it, since the other two were down by her feet. I had requested they send positive healing energy to her. As I continued to lay hands on her forehead, to my shock the forehead bruise disappeared. No one had seen the bruise except me, so I was comfortable with the secret. I have never repeated that result. It always seemed like a bit too much of a miracle worker for me. Remember I am the white chick from Tacoma, not a guru in India.

After Maria was feeling better, we had lunch and then it was my turn. They told me my Mayan name is Two Storm. My joy and life's work should be to help people through their storms of life. When they told me this, I smiled–for that *has* been my life's work. After that day, we became heart-connected friends. Later I would travel to Mexico with our friend Carol to visit with them and visit with the pyramids.

Thoughts about the Pyramids

My first connections with the pyramids happened when I was a child. Who built the pyramids and why were they built? Were the pyramids in Egypt and in Central and South America connected, and if they were connected how were they connected? All ideas for a child's mind to ponder. Most likely you also thought about these things. Now, there is much more information. We know through research that cultures in both places saw a connection with earth-sky. Both saw the pyramids as sacred. The Central and South American pyramids resemble structurally the Mesopotamia temples in the Middle East, more than in Egypt. As we learn more about our ancient ancestors through DNA chromosome research, establishing the nature of the migrating populations, we understand that shared mythology, and building techniques are certainly possible.

People have always been travelers, or at least some people. They may have moved because of warring factions, or drought, or farming land becoming a desert. Based on current observations of the global populations, some people like to travel and some people love the adventure of new lands and customs. Some move to improve their prosperity. Some people move for education. Each group bring their own cultural ideas with them.

The other possibility is people have a common innate awareness and belief system. This innate ability wants to acknowledge the connection between the earth and the sky, an intuitive awareness of the energetic connection force. They want to honor this knowledge with a structure.

Modern techniques allow engineers to develop advances to build taller and taller buildings. Most are not a pyramid shape but some are. Some people have felt that building tall buildings is a way to superimpose human control on life. It certainly is a dominant statement in the sky. In a culture of hierarchical statements tall buildings are important, such as the penthouse suite, or which floor your office is located in a building (third floor is less impressive than the forty-second). Another possibility is this: at higher altitudes, according to the law of physics, time is faster. If time is faster there, is it the bridge to another dimension? Are people blocking their own paranormal abilities when they think that they have to work hard and use a tool? Most indigenous cultures know that to experience paranormal events only takes openness to the ability, and reassurance that this is part of the normal human experience.

Mexico: Aztec Story

A few years later my friend Carol and I went to Mexico to visit Sonia and Maria. Carol goes to Mexico at least once a year and speaks Spanish very well. An ideal traveling companion! We landed in Mexico City and stayed a few days with our friends. Later we went to Cuernavaca, the city of Springtime. I heard about the healing techniques used by some curanderos in their practices. A curandero is a folk medicine healer in Mexico. All three of my friends seek out alterative healing methods. The trip was rich with discussion and our friends pampered us. Maria's sister was gone traveling and she had offered Maria her chauffer to take us around. The chauffeur had a story of his own. He had worked for Anheuser-Busch, the beer company, taking care of their famous Clydesdale horses. He had returned to Mexico to help with the care of his aging parents. He missed the horses but enjoyed driving for a living too. Mexico City has congested streets; it is an immense city. Fabulously wonderful to have an experienced driver. He also was a bit of a tour guide, although Carol and our friends were knowledgeable too.

The next day, Maria had arranged for the same driver with her sister's car to chauffeur Carol and me to Teotihuacan, an ancient pyramid site about

25 miles north of Mexico City. Here was the magic of history. It is a huge compound with two outstanding pyramids in particular. The Pyramid of the Sun has super many steps and it really is an exercise of merit to get to the top of the pyramid. Totally worth it! It had a wonderful spiritual feel to it. The view was spectacular seeing for miles and seeing all of the huge compound. The energy felt sacred and light. Upon inquiring we were told a group of Tibetan monks had recently come through, and did a special ceremony of clearing and blessing for this pyramid. The Pyramid of the Sun is recognized as the masculine pyramid in the compound. The female pyramid is called the Pyramid of the Moon. It is a smaller pyramid located at the other end of the site.

We walked to the Pyramid of the Moon. Half way to this pyramid, the chauffer seemed to magically appear. I believe he had water for us and offered to take our packages. We have bought some items from local craftspeople. It was such a pamper and I wonder how he knew when to meet us. The timing was perfect. We had not discussed it and Carol appeared as surprised as I was. Later, I realized that he was intuitive knower. When we arrived at the pyramid, I was expecting the same quality of light energy. To my dismay, it had heavy energy and the energy felt stuck. After pondering why, I realized, "the why" was not as important as recognizing this was my energetic clearing service work. Oh, it started to make sense: the Tibetan monks focused on the masculine. It made sense that I focus on the sacred feminine energy. First, there was an inner eye-popping feeling of "But it is just me, and not a group of people." I reminded myself that Carol was with me and she would help in any way possible. I reminded myself how powerful female sacred medicine is. Also, I reminded myself the Universe/God has my back. If it were supposed to be more than just Carol and me, it would be. I prayed. Next, I made some small vortexes to clear the energy. As we walked through the pyramid, our plan was to cocreate a shift and dissipate the heavy energy, replacing it with light loving energy. Carol offered her intention and prayers. Next, I opened the top area of the pyramid to receive the love of the universe. The plan was, this would keep a constant flow of higher vibration energy in the pyramid and open the connection of the pyramid to the moon's energy.

Often after a huge clearing there is a confirming sign from the universe. In this situation, the confirming sign touched my heart. Some Aztecs had come to the site to perform a ceremony. One of the young females was having a naming ceremony honoring her passage into the beginnings of womanhood. Everyone was dressed in traditional attire. We were asked along with others to witness the ceremony and to participate in the dancing. After the naming ceremony gifts were distributed, not unlike the naming ceremony practices I had attended in the Pacific Northwest. My gift was an agave cactus fruit. Agave fruit is sweet on the inside—sweet heart and disposition. Eat too much and it will give you the runs—remember moderation. It has a protective cover on the outside—use your boundaries to protect yourself. Great advice for all of us, but particularly a young female beginning her life as a woman. Three interesting events happened on our way home from Mexico. First, we sat next to a computer whiz, that had been visiting her family in Mexico City. I talked to her about the energetic work and the naming ceremony. She was very interested, and told me her brother-in-law was a Native American from Arizona, followed the medicine path ways, and had moved to Mexico to be with and married her sister. He was involved with the Aztec sacred traditions and participated. She was sure he and others would want to hear about the energetic work for the Pyramid of the Moon. In some Native American circles this method is referred to with a smile and a chuckle as the Indian telegraph system. News travel faster than the person with the original story, much faster. Second, I forgot agave was a fruit, besides a ceremonial gift. For some reason, customs let me keep it. I was very clear in my own mind it was a ceremonial gift and I was supposed to bring it to the USA. It was much more than a plain cactus fruit. Years later, I thought how did I do that? Lastly, I lost my journal, detailing the trip. I think I must have left it on the plane but I am not sure. It is one of the few journals and maybe the only journal I have lost. It was for my memory to remember not my pen and paper.

Mexico: Mayan Chichen-Itza

The first pyramid I touched was in Chichen-Itza. The year was around 1980. I remember the Great North Platform, the Temple Warriors, the Great Ball Court, the Sacrifice of the Virgin site. And mostly I remember climbing and climbing those stairs. My depth perception is slightly off so I decided to go down the steep stairs on my bottom. All of a sudden I screamed— something had bit me and I jumped to my feet. As I jumped up I saw a scorpion scurry back inside a crack in the stairwell. Of course, I was scared. Was I going to get really sick? Of course, I took the tactic of "wait and see." Luckily at the time I had a lot of muscle there. The sting only numbed the area and it just felt weird for a couple of days. I hope the scorpion lived to dash another day.

I remember the Ball Court and how I imagined different towns coming to compete with each other. It seemed like such a normal non-exotic detail of their life. I could relate to running or watching the games. It also for some reason reminded me of the Olympics, a peaceful way to show skill and dominance, comradery with each other and respect for the players' abilities. I just sat and tried to visualize a real game. Upon doing some research later, I was reminded the blood and gore of the games, pictures depicting blood and beheading. The Sacrifice Pool site, and the sacrificial altar on the top of the giant pyramid, were too difficult for me to begin to comprehend as to why of these events. How did this practice become normalized in their society? Was it considered the lesser of two evils, one sacrificed for the greater good? Was it a fear tactic to intimidate families, or was it an honor to be selected to die for your people? I do not know.

I do know that I was very impressed with the jaguar and the feathered serpent in the culture. Both of these animals I hold dear to my heart. The jaguars for their sleekness, beauty, athleticism and prowess. The feathered serpents because I love dragon mythology and have even written a story about Dazzle Dragon. Dragon represents a four-post balance for me, walk on the earth, fly in the sky, swim in the water and breathe fire for truth. My automobile's name is Green Dragon.

At Chichen-Itza, they also have an underground tunnel system and a building that resembles the sacred tree of their myths. The tree of life. Another, how cool is that moment?

This trip, no energetic magic happened unless you consider my connection with the scorpion and swimming in the beautiful warm blue sea. However, it was significant to me to really be present, and walk the steps of the pyramids, and the pathways within the city. Mindful of how many people have walked these paved paths in their everyday life long ago. It was a humbling historical event for me of time and antiquity. I felt like a witness to their past. Also, it was impressive to be reminded of the superior knowledge of the Mayans. They understood astronomy, and how to use their building much like the makers of Stonehenge did many moons ago.

AH HA Moments

Having the courage to accept the notion, *Change is Always Constant*. When was change not a part of our lives? When do we begin to hate change, and need to control change? Is change the root of the issue, or is it our feelings about something else? Have we used "I hate change" to really mask some other feelings? For instance, changing school and missing your friends, fear of new surroundings, new friends, and possibly a new school, is not the actual change action. Change happens minute by minute, hour by hour. Mostly, we like to change our clothes so change is not always a negative experience in our daily lives. Does change exist before judgment? Not always, sometimes it is the future potential action, rather than the actual change.

Indigenous Healers/ Teachers

The method of a teacher is to watch and learn. As a student watches and learns, a path appears to be followed through talent, dedication and dreams. Young people are surrounded by elders who can guide them to their assorted intuitive talents and abilities. For instance, I once knew a medicine shaman woman, a very honorable respected elder. Others told me she had a connection to honey bees, her spiritual power animal. People who knew her said they had seen bees swarm her, and cover her body with themselves. She was never stung during these encounters. Rather, it was an acknowledged physical connection; she was a part of their swarm or family. A person may receive a connective knowing about a power animal from an elder shaman, or during a dream or meditation. This receiving person honors their connection, and ideally, once a month, they do their power animal dance, influenced by the moon's cycle. Prophecy dreams and interpreting them is part of maturation into life.

Lucky for many of us, the indigenous groups have kept their awareness of the paranormal as a normal human ability, like singing or dancing. Lucky for us that some of the indigenous medicine people and shamans shared their knowledge with outsiders. Their sharing with outsiders were often looked upon with suspicion by their community. Some did not trust or respect non-natives to honor the teachings. No matter what culture you belong to, some people are not trustworthy. Many Native American prophecies talk about how Native Americans will be the teachers for a new generation of people. The prophecies state that this new generation of people are reincarnated from a previous Native American life and have respect for the teachings imprinted on their souls. Certainly, more and more people appreciate Native American wisdom. Is it a coincidence that global populations are standing with the Native Americans at Standing Rock for the Earth's water? Or, is it that the conscience and conscious awareness have risen to a new level of participation? This participation is motivated by the deep heart connection of love.

AH HA Moments

> Many of us LOVE our planet. To me that is
> the good news.

Earth Is Our Nurturer

Rocks Help Heal

Many of us are drawn to rocks and like rocks very much. When I was young, I learned that rocks were inanimate objects and had no life force. I soaked the information up and believed it. An adult, most likely more than one adult, had told me that and it seemed reasonable. After all, rocks did not have eyes or ears or mouths to talk. They must not be living. As I have aged, my definition of "living" has changed. Now I ask, does this something have an energetic force? If it has an energetic force, it has a life force. My teachers in the Native American traditions taught me that some rocks are ancient and carry the ancient wisdom of the earth.

I decided to hold a rock in my hand and try to communicate with it. It was possible. Again, this is through telepathy and not speaking words. Rocks have all kinds of thoughts about people, and for people. Also, each rock has its own chemical component and is unique. I love going to the beach and walking the beach looking at the rocks.

Sometimes I feel compelled to pick up a rock. It might have really good energy and it feels wonderful to hold it. Or, I might send the rock divine healing energy because it wanted a little boost. Some rocks want to go with you, others definitely want to stay in place. I have had rocks ask to go with me and after a short period of time want to be placed in a new location. Do I know why the rock wanted to move? Sometimes, but it is not my main concern. My concern is being of service. Rocks have been around a lot longer than people, and they are my elders to respect.

People have studied minerals and rocks and find that different minerals and rocks help in different situations. For instance, rose quartz is a wonderful rock for love, and can help a person's heart heal by placing the rock on the chest of the affected person.

During my studies with Native Americans and learning about their medicine path way, I was taught to dig a hole and place all the heavy emotional feelings into the earth for cleansing and clearing. This is a common practice. As my own abilities developed, I had an insight during one of my meditations. One of my new energetic tasks was to take the heavy energy from the earth and send it somewhere else. I do this through telepathically communicating with the earth; I knew the earth was hurting on so many different levels. She did not want to die, but her ability to give was waning. She is suffering from all the years of people taking from her and not giving back. We called her Mother Earth, and yet much of the focus has been on her generosity towards us, not on our responsibility and respect towards her. I am not sure the earth is a she. I believe the earth in her balanced state is an evolved soul, a complete balance of male and female without the identification of gender. Is it another coincidence that, as the earth becomes more balanced, transgender populations and their need for recognition have surfaced?

When I first began clearing our earth, my impulse was to direct the heavy energy by using a hose to send it into the earth's atmosphere. After doing this a few times, it occurred to me that now I was polluting the sky and not solving the problem. I knew enough about energy to know that it did not just evaporate. Someone might be flying in a plane, go through it and be affected. The next step was to send it outside our atmosphere. Again, was this really safe for others? Space travel is possible. What about the potential to do harm to non-earth people? The answer came to me—was it in meditation, or just reading about black holes? I do not remember. I directed this heavy dense energy to a black hole. Sending this heavy dense energy to a black hole is the safest way to dispose of it.

Recently scientists have changed their mind that black holes do not contain moisture. They have found one black hole that does seem to have moisture. I wondered. Many cultures view emotions as water. Is the potential finding of water in a black hole the result of all those heavy emotions going to my designated black hole? I have not pursued it, but it is an interesting topic to explore. What exactly is a *Black Hole*?

Black Holes

"A black hole is a place in space where gravity pulls so much that even light cannot get out. The gravity is so strong because matter has been squeezed into a tiny space. This can happen when a star is dying.

Because no light can get out, people can't see black holes. They are invisible. Space telescopes with special tools can help find black holes. The special tools can see how stars that are very close to black holes act differently than other stars.

Black holes can be big or small. Scientists think the smallest black holes are as small as just one atom. These black holes are very tiny but have the mass of a large mountain. Mass is the amount of matter, or "stuff," in an object.

Another kind of black hole is

called "stellar." Its' mass can be up to 20 times more than the mass of the sun. There may be many, many stellar mass black holes in Earth's galaxy. Earth's galaxy is called the Milky Way."[1]

I believe in the study of science. My son is a research scientist and my mother was a chemist. Science is a great gateway to knowledge. This book is not science; rather it is made up of my own observations. When I look at the action of a black hole I see female energy. Why female energy?

Black holes use the creative force of female energy, much like the sexual act producing an offspring. Matter enters the womb and returns in a different form or it is absorbed into a woman's body. It is very powerful energy and the ancients understood the awesomeness of women's power. We are also learning more and more about this.

---

[1] http://www.nasa.gov/audience/forstudents/k-4/stories/nasa-knows/what-is-a-black-hole-k4.html

AH HA Moments

Dancing Is life! Everybody get out there and dance. Or get up now and dance a few steps. It is one of the best way to honor our body's joy.

The 18th and 21st Dimensions

A few years ago, I realized that I was not meeting with other energetic workers and my social life had narrowed. I wanted to connect again with people working in this field. I joined a couple of groups and started to dialogue with people about their work. It was at this time I realized that my abilities were unusual. I remember other practitioners asking me how I did this or that. I remember people wondering if I was exaggerating; it confused me.

As practitioners, we decided to trade services to experience each other's energetic work. When it was my turn to do a treatment session other practitioners exclaimed, "Your work is amazing! How do you do that?" I was surprised by this but finally I heard this message. I had heard that message from others but I had discounted it as flattery. These people were also practitioners, with no need to flatter me. Rather, I sensed their sincerity about their words.

One of the practitioners talked to us about his psychic abilities, and how he was a channeler of beings from other vibrational dimensions. He said his spirit guides told him he was working within the 15th Dimension. His guides told him it is the Diamond Level. I had never thought about dimensions when I did my energetic work. I thought to myself what a good idea to ask. So, I asked in one of meditations, "Am I working on the Diamond Level too?" I felt like this energetic worker understood me more than some people. The answer I heard in my meditation was "No, you work on the platinum level and you work within the 18th and 21st Dimensions." First, I looked up platinum and read that platinum is considered more valuable than diamond. Next, I looked up 21st Dimension and found a scientific paper from a scientist talking about the 21st Dimension. He said the

21st dimension is the vibration of the universe and is the vibration of pure love.[2]

Now I decided to explore further. When I googled the 18th Dimension it said the planet Earth vibrates on the 18th Dimension. Unfortunately, I did not find it when I googled it again. I did find some New Age type articles about the 18th dimension.

The Earth-Sky Connection jogged my memory. Years ago, at a weekend energetic healing workshop I met a woman. She came up to me and said. "Who are you?" I told her my name. She said, "No, I am not talking about your name, I am talking about your energy field. Your energy is Earth-Sky," I started to cry because no one had ever truly seen me before and it felt wonderful. Still, I was not ready to be seen by all. I tucked the information in my brain and periodically thought about it. On an intuitive level, I have always known who I am. On an

---

[2]
http://adsabs.harvard.edu/abs/2009APS..MAR.S1104 L, consulted 1/16/17.

emotional level, I was not ready to accept myself with my talents and spiritual gifts. I felt my life was not exotic enough for me to be me.

This diamond level practitioner gave me a session. What happened next confirmed my meditation information. I was to lie down and listen to his words. I believe the idea was to put me in a theta brain wave state. We both hung up the phone and we both connected on a higher vibration waking-dream state. The first realization I had was I was in a clay kiva. A rounded-top door was the only entrance to the kiva. We went inside and the side went up at a gentle angle to the top of the cone. At the top of the cone was a circular opening. At first I was comfortable and felt like we were clearing some things. After a short while, I felt very confined there. I started flying all around the walls, almost bouncing off them. I wanted to leave. Finally, I realized I could go out the door and fly away. After I flew out, I headed for the stars. It was a marvelous feeling I felt wild and free, and I was so enjoying flying through the universe. It was and is still one of my best memories. The phone rang, and it was the practitioner wondering if I had fallen asleep. The session had ended 15 minutes earlier, and I had not called back as per our agreement. My phone alarm clock had not sounded. I was a little embarrassed, just a little, to admit I was having so much fun I lost track of the time. After the session, we discussed it. The practitioner told me he pictured us in a clay kiva. He said that I reminded him of a little fairy because I kept darting all around. He said he did not get any significant past-life readings, which was unusual. He said I darted out the door and went up and up. He followed me out the door and was trying to catch me but I kept going up and up and finally he had to turn around and return to the kiva. I never returned to the kiva.

It confirmed to me that he is indeed a very capable clear-vision practitioner. He most likely does work within the 15th dimension and my work is most likely within the 18th-21st dimension. This idea is based on both our observations of our session together.

AH HA Moments

My inner and outer core work can be a difficult process. Sometimes our outer core will be hard work because our inner core is crying for attention. It is all good. My inner core work is honed by my meditation practice. My meditation mind might sometimes be noisy with thoughts but it gives me an understanding as to what is going on with me. It is a quiet reflection of self-analysis with the help of your own energy field, guiding you to join with the energy field of the universe. Sometimes, my outer world is so busy my inner world does not get to have a voice. Meditation gives it that voice. That chatter in my head can be hidden with all the busy-action-packed-to-do list of daily lives. This was especially true when I was a single mom raising my son. Things I have noticed, when my inner core changes my outer core changes too, and it is easier to maintain some order. As I heal, my own home becomes more decluttered and orderly.

Shine the Light on Evil

As I began my psychic energy classes I was almost immediately called to work on the dark side to shine the light on evil. My teacher was not pleased with this development, but was supportive of what was being asked of me. She reminded me to keep myself in protection. She said I had the talent to be helpful to others. Being of service to others has always been important to me; this felt like a way to serve.

Of course, predators exist in this world. Part of my criminal justice job was working with people classified as predators. Yes, some of them had committed heinous acts but they were still people, and as you know people are a mixed bag of good and evil. I had learned through my training as an anthropologist to be observant of behavior. This was not a matter of knowing WHY someone does something. It was a be-a-witness WATCH training to be able to professionally step back, and observe without condemning. When I take that step, my own energetic vibration maintained a higher love vibration and shielded me from evil. Low vibration evil cannot attach itself to a higher vibration of love. The lower dense vibration has trouble staying so evil, because its energy is now mixing with the energy of love.

One of the ways I helped was dowsing, or searching for the names of potential victims, and through mental telepathy, warning them they were in danger. Then, I could put them in a protective light.

In my experience, there are two types of evil predators. The first one is environmental. A person is raised with so much punishment, humiliation and violence they create a secret life of rage. They feel helpless to stop their environmental abuse and a secret fantasy life makes things easier. Sometimes, this fantasy rage becomes so powerful they decide to act on their impulses. These are the people who make the news. This is one of the reasons I am a strong advocate of early childhood education. This diversifies a child's experience in their early life. It also may help a parent to seek help for themselves. Isolation is not the same thing as solitude.

The second type of predator, is a person with a walk-in. A side note, not all walk-ins have evil intention; more about walk-ins later in the book. A predator walk-in is evil and preys on living human beings, using them to house their spirit. I believe until recently Jack the Ripper's soul was wandering the earth. He found a human, was able to walk in to the body, and he continues his gruesome acts of murder. The danger with killing a known serial killer is by their death the spirit is now free to roam to find another body. However, this person is not known to the police, and it may take years to capture the new serial killer; same evil spirit on a killing spree. Yes, I believe I had an interaction with Jack the Ripper's spirit and moved him along to his next level of experience. By mixing a higher vibration with the lower vibration, two things happen. One, the lower vibration entity does not like the sound of a light higher vibration. Two, with an additional level of love vibration they are more willing to change to a different frequency. Love heals.

Do devils really exist? Yes, in my experience they do. Not all evil entities are the devil but, devils are all evil. Energetically they feel different and they look different. Exorcisms are necessary to help people regain their own personhood. I have cleared three or four devils from people. Look into a person's eyes, a devil around divine love will form a raging bull look in the eye. Again, some of the earlier medieval mystic artists knew this. They depicted the devil with features of a bull.

I was psychically attacked at times. It is not pleasant! I have felt big globs of a dark tarlike substance thrown at me. I have felt people trying to attach themselves to my energy, rather than using the energy of their own heart, chakras and soul. They are doing a disservice to themselves, because it is a much more joyful connection with source and body as a direct experience, less complicated, maybe even much less complicated.

Soul Retrieval

Soulless people are people who are just the opposite of a walk-in. They have no spirit within them. As we are taught, the eyes are the window of the soul. Have you ever noticed someone who has dead eyes or lifeless eyes? Yet they function without any apparent problems. They go to their job, might play games, and be involved with life's activities. However, when you look into their eyes, it is almost a vacant stare. People talk and wonder about soul retrieval. Yes, soul retrieval is a viable method to reconnect this person with their soul spirit. Soul retrieval is also a great way to return parts of you that have splintered off. Who knew, right? There are assorted energetic workers that can help with this reconnection with self. It is delicate work so trust you gut in finding the right person to guide you.

The first time I participated in a soul retrieval session I was a skeptical client. Was this something or was it just make-believe? There was drumming, lots of noise and chanting. I was not really relaxed. The longer the drumming lasted, though, the more I relaxed. All of a sudden I remembered a memory of myself as a child. I had completely forgotten about the traumatic feeling of that interaction. It all came flooding back with lots of emotion, young vulnerable emotion. I was told to breathe as I cried. As I remember it took me a couple days to feel balanced again. However, this time I felt more complete as person, more solid as if a part of me returned to me. I found it fascinating, and so helpful, and I learned more of who I am.

Years ago, I was in Tacoma at Point Defiance Park. I decided to walk around the grounds near the entrance. My intuition guided me to stop at a certain place. All of a sudden I was flooded with old memories of a perceived wrong. I was so mad and had completely forgotten about the incident. I had done soul retrieval through drumming and someone had facilitated my reconnection. This felt like the same thing only without the drumming or facilitator. It was just me on the grass at a local park. I went home and wrote about my long-gone feelings. Apparently, part of me left because I was not willing to stand up for myself. I would stand up for other people but not myself. When I did not stand up for myself I felt resentful and powerless. This part of my soul would have none of that and left. I remember having a conversation in my mind's eye with that part of myself. I had to promise to take better care of her needs if she was staying. So, I promised. Have I always kept this promise? MMMM, probably not, but it is something I am very aware of now and awareness is more than half the battle.

AH HA Moments

In our culture, we have an indirect way of blaming something other than the root cause of the problem. As if by acknowledging the root cause the pain will increase. Is it the dualistic nature of the Western mind? Seeking to separate from pain instead of embracing it as a life cycle.

Sometimes to minimize our feelings we make excuses for others who seem like ourselves. Or we maximize our fear or anger. We judge others harshly if they are not like us, or we judge others harshly because they are like us. The dualistic nature of us vs them. How about being a witness to the action and staying focused on feelings about the interaction?

Change—sometimes we force a change on others that may not be necessary. It might be us who need to change.

Tempted: Return to Darkness

A temptation came into my life. I shared office space in a lovely healing center. Most of us had other professions (facials, craniosacral therapy, medicine, and acupuncture) but we were also energy workers. We did have some turnover. One new officemate was an energy worker and somehow, I became competitive with her. Not sure she ever knew. She bragged about being an energy healer working with Crow energy. I felt jealous because I did work with Crow energy but had felt a strong intuitive message to stop going into the darkness. In Native American mythology, Crow brings the light to the darkness. My competitive nature drove me to decide I could again work with Crow energy. My envy of someone else's path guided me to return to my previous road of bringing light to the darkness. My first thought was "This is *my* job!" As you can observe my pesky fragile ego was in charge.

Within a couple of weeks, or it might have been days, I was given a message to stop this behavior. I was walking along the Burke-Gilman trail in Seattle. This trail is miles long and is a walking and bike path. It has many trees and views of Lake Washington, sometimes only a peek-a-boo view. The property previously belonged to the railroad and it had railroad tracks. The local government took over the trail and took out the railroad tracks and put down an asphalt road about 7 feet wide. Depending on the time of day it can be a meditative walk with nature and sounds of birds chirping. As I walked along, all of a sudden, a black crow dropped from a tree and landed one or two feet from me. It was either dead already or died right after it hit the ground. A young blond woman walking from the opposite direction had seen the incident and commented on it. She had never seen anything like it. We talked about it being a sign and she was sure it was, but had no idea what it meant. I knew what it meant. The crow medicine path was dead for me.

I did not share my own recent behavior shift of returning to the dark side to save others. To say I felt bad is an understatement. If I had only listened to my inner guidance maybe that crow would not have had to make such a dramatic statement about my spiritual path. It motivated me to get back to my own energetic work and put my heart into the pursuit of bringing lightness to this planet.

The Highway Almost-Mishap

In 2014, a group of Seattle area friends were traveling to the Oregon town of Bend to see another friend that had moved there. She had been raised in Oregon and wanted to return to her roots. Part of the visit was so our friend Liz could show us the beautiful countryside. Liz offered to drive and we all piled into her car to see the sites. The sites were beautiful. We went to the forest. As part of our nature adventure tour we went up a mountain pass. The tall alpine trees were gorgeous. The road was solidly paved and we felt secure as we traveled along it. There was a steep incline to one side. The road was mostly a two-lane highway with little or no traffic. Isolated, really. As we traveled, periodically an extra passing lane was available for a short distance. This helped keep the road less congested, and gave the slower traffic an opportunity to move to the right.

The passing lane were soon narrowing to our one lane of the two-lane highway. Liz, not wanting to get behind a big truck, decided to pass it. She had plenty of time, we had the extra passing lane, and she speeded up a little to get by the truck. To our surprise and then horror the truck would not let us pass, rather the truck picked up speed, and started to move into our lane seemingly to push us off the road. Liz blasted her horn. The truck kept coming. Yes, the intention was clear; to push us off the road, remember we are in the wilderness with a steep bank next to the road. If danger arrives my first impulse is to put people and a vehicle in white light to stop the attack. To my shock this truck was extremely powerful and was using an energetic force to push back. I had to use all of my energetic strength to keep us off the bank, and on the road. I called in my angels of light. The result was a push-pull wind-like action. With all my energetic muscle, I used my karate word breath to give me more strength. Liz continued to drive with courage. She saw our danger. She gunned the engine and we raced away. We just made it! The road was once again a two-lane highway, and the opposite flow of ongoing traffic was coming towards us. We never saw the face of the driver. We never saw the truck again.

Liz said it felt and reminded her of a movie of a soulless driver, or even a driverless truck and all you could see was the grill of the truck. Pure evil was coming from that truck. Yes, this was no ordinary driver. I felt the intention to push us off the road and the pure evil of this behavior. Previously, I have worked with violent offenders and have witnessed human rage. This was not an ordinary person. This was not even a person hopped up on drugs. Rather this was a very evil spirit wanting to do us harm. Years later it occurred to me that I was the target of this pure evil entity. Wow, what if "it" knew the work I had been quietly doing for the earth, and really knew before I did that my cocreative work would be more public and global. This was not my first brush with evil spirits but this one was fiercer than any others I have felt. The target was me. Very grateful for all my guardian angels and the healing light of God's love or the universe's love. People who read my energy field have told me that I have at least 20 guardian angels. They are amazed. Why would anyone need so many? However, having had narrow escapes such as the story above, I always smile and say and "Yes, and I need all of them!"

AH HA Moments

Criticism is only helpful to me if it given with a loving, supportive heart. When someone criticizes me and it feels like bullying I do not like it. It is important to find your own rhythm in your life to be at ease with yourself.

The Body Talks

DNA Memories

Scientists are discovering that we can carry through inherited DNA, genetic memories of our ancestors. As an energetic worker, I have sensed this exact phenomenon in people. Your ancestor on your mother's side four generations ago almost drowned, and this created a fear of drowning. Or, they may have witnessed a drowning and created a fear of others drowning. You inherited this genetic memory. So, you might fear your own drowning or the people around you drowning. Hence, you may not like to go to the water for recreation.

Or, two siblings have a near-drowning experience when their canoe flips in a river. One recovers quickly from the incident, recognizing accidents happen. The other sibling becomes very traumatized and seeks therapy. Perhaps the second person inherited a dominant memory of an ancestor's fear of drowning, but this ancestral DNA memory is not inherited by the other descendent. The second person has the recent experience and the ancestor's experience to process. It might be only an accident, but two accidents, especially one that produced unprocessed, emotional, ancestral trauma memories, and are not as easy to brush off as an isolated occurrence. The additional trauma memory may not be recognized as the root of the reaction. The focus being on the most recent event. As the helping profession know more about genetics, they recognize this factor as a potential phenomenon of their clients.

Past Life Connections

For myself I have had a fear of drowning most of my life. Years ago, a man and I were on the same computer group Listserve. We got to know each other and had instant connection/crush. As we emailed, I learned he had a fear of drowning too. One day I had this vision that we had known each other and both died drowning when a ship went down. We had vowed to find each other again. My vision resonated with him too. It was a knowing familiar feeling. We all have feelings like that. By finding each other, talking it through, and clearing the memory, we completed our vow to each other. After the clearing, we drifted apart, our work together done. He lived in Australia, we only met through email, he was married with a family and so it was not for us to really know each other. Rather it was for us to help heal each other, dissolve the vow, and the fear of drowning. In this life, it was not a relationship to move forward, but it did change my view of past life beliefs. My fear of downing was reduced to a minor anxiety.

Another time I was working with a client. She was having trouble with her right shoulder or neck and wanted energetic work. During the session, a strong image of a pair of boots came up. The boots appeared to be worn by an Asian soldier, an infantryman. All of a sudden I was transported back to a sacred temple. Many monks were on the floor and had been praying and meditating. The door burst open and soldiers flooded into the room armed with rifles. The soldier with the boots was now part of this terrible scene of killing. The person viewing the shoes appeared to be a monk. He was killed by the soldier. It was a quick death but a shock to the body. The client experienced the exact same vision. Neither one of us had a good explanation except it was a past life experience. After that day, I again believed in the possibilities of past lives. After clearing the memory of the emotional shock of the unexpected death, the client's physical problem ended. She was not of Asian ancestry so it did not appear to be a DNA memory.

Fear of Flying

Fear of flying is not that uncommon. I have worked with two clients with this fear. Their fears looked the same to the outside world. They exhibited some of the same symptoms of anxiety, shortness of breath, tightening of the chest, eyes filled with, *what if.* Both used avoidance, meaning they flew as little as they could, or medicated themselves. However, the inside world of each was very different. The first client, Jamie, grew up with this fear. The most remarkable part of this story is she is from a different country and has lived in multiple cities in Europe, Africa and now in the USA. Many of us are not that adventurous, and surely, she knew flying was a part of the equation of a geographic change. Yet, her adventurous spirit was more vital and alive than her fear. She came to me as a middle-aged woman, wanting some relief. We cocreated a session together. She did have some fear of flying in her DNA memories. This memory began much earlier before planes were common in the sky. It is possible that her ancestors heard the words from their parents, people do not fly. This belief was challenged by seeing planes in the air during World War I. Thus, introducing the startling idea that people can fly with the right machine. What a concept! On the flip side, the fear belief was also strengthened by neighborhood chit-chat about planes crashing, and pilots either dying or being hurt. Some of the stories were told with extra drama for the myth-story. Another factor was also present. As a young child, she was often with a dearly beloved aunt. This aunt was an amazing woman but had anxiety issues around flying. She bubbled over with this anxiety. My client is an empath. Empaths are people that have the ability to pick up others' energy.

I do believe all of us have this ability and here is an example. Have you ever listened to someone's tale of woe and afterwards felt completely drained, tired and had a mood change? The person telling the tale of woe mentions how much better they feel, so much lighter. They thank you and off they go. Meantime, your happy, joyous state is now compromised, and you need a nap, beer or a walk/run. If you have, chances are you are an empath. Just as with so many talents, some empaths have more ability than others. My client loved her aunt so much that she felt all her fears about flying. She knew she could help and absorbed her aunt's heavy emotions. The good news is her aunt lived her life less anxious, but the bad news is my client became much more prone to anxiety, especially about flying. She was three years old when she made this decision. Three-year-olds do not have the abstract mental reasoning to figure out the long-term effects of absorbing someone else's energy. Many children are concrete thinkers with open hearts. They live in the now. If you notice a change in your child's behavior when they are around certain people, make sure you add a cup of Epsom salt to their bath water. This helps clear the daily energy of others. Oh, and it also helps adults to clear their energy field. Adults can use more, say two cups of Epsom salt. Another alternative method is baking soda in the tub. Of course, my favorite way is a swim in warm salt water. It never happens enough in my life. I live in the Pacific Northwest and I am content to mostly wade in our lovely sea water.

Back to the story. This cocreative session required the client to want to clear her long held anxiety and cocreate with me energetically. As many of you know, people put up barriers. Have you ever tried to tell someone something and they did not hear your words? They become defensive, or change the subject, or just passively listen without absorbing the idea. Only months later, they tell you their new insight, and it is what you have been telling them for months if not years. People are ready to change only when they are ready, a free will choice. That is the good news and the bad news. Since, I am people I do it too, and probably will continue to do it. I think it is called the human adventure.

Returning to my client's session. We cleared her DNA memories. After that, I saw this woman standing close to a female relative as a young child. This woman was very fun to be with, but also anxious. My client immediately recognized her as a wonderful aunt that she dearly loved. Since the heavy energy was never the client's own feelings, it was an easy liftoff removal. As a visual, think of spilling a drink all over yourself. You will need a cleanup on the outside of your body and possibly a new dry outfit but no permanent damage. The permanent damage comes if a person internalizes it as a trauma event, such as someone purposely throwing a drink on you to show their displeasure. Later, during a follow-up I talked with my client. She reported no further problems when she flew.

The second client had some DNA memories about fear of flying and no memories, or any energetic fear familial attachments in this lifetime.

She was traveling to Europe with her family soon and did not want the discomfort. She emailed from Iceland to tell me that the first leg of the trip her anxiety was better but she was still having some fears. For her, it was important she leaned into her fear and be actively engaged as a warrior. When she did this, the fear dissipated and she had no more problems.

We are all such unique people. I love this about all of us.

AH HA Moments

In my life, I have been quick to be stimulated by my outer environment. I have spent much of my life on hyper-alert. Was this because my father had occasional rages or was it the way my DNA entered this world? It is probably both. Being on hyper-alert cued me to my surroundings and to people's behavior. If someone's behavior broke their traditional movement pattern, I noticed. When I was younger, I became upset when others did not acknowledge what I was observing. It was only years later that I realized not everyone could sense what I can. I remember in first grade we had four sets of twins. People had trouble telling them apart but I never did. To me they looked very different, and I did not understand why others said they could not tell them apart. We all have different abilities and talents. I did not really understand that when I was six years old. It was just one big puzzle thought to me.

Working with Elders

Solving My Social Anxiety

I had developed some social anxiety, and was starting to feel uncomfortable around new people experiences. The best way to diminish these feelings for me is to be active socially. Slowly I felt myself withdrawing. This also affected my self-employment. Some of my friends were concerned about my lack of earning money, and my withdrawal, such as at a party or a summer picnic. They urged me to find a part-time job.

Needing to Heal the Past

I applied for the job as a part-time receptionist at a retirement community. After some campaigning I was given the job. My boss was not sure that I would stay or it would be a good fit.

Honestly, while I had done some receptionist work in my life it was more to relieve someone for 15 minutes (not exactly super experienced) plus, I was going through thyroid fog brain and menopause (not exactly good candidate for training). Learned lots, how to count money especially change, how to clear a copy machine clog, and most importantly; receptionists do not have any social status in an organization. I went from being considered an expert in different areas, almost guru status, to having people say, "How would you know that?" It was a mind bender for me. My family was one of the most intellectual families in my childhood neighborhood, so people expected that I knew stuff even when I didn't.

Another reason I wanted the job was because both of my parents had died when I was fairly young, and thus stopped some of the history I needed to process my childhood. These people were my parents' peers, and on occasion, I would meet someone who knew my parents. Mostly I was trying to figure out what behavior was my family's attitudes and traditions, and what came from our social class. As a free spirit artist type, some everyday life structures confused me and I wanted to know more. We were upper middle class but we lived in an area that had many wealthy people. We moved to this area when I was almost nine. Prior to that we lived in a blue-collar neighborhood so I was also comfortable with people who prided themselves on their intelligent hands to fix or make things. Plus, both sides of the family had a long history of farming. I did not know until after my mother moved to California that she and my dad had some social class anxiety about their own place in our neighborhood. Another part was I have a curious mind and a degree in anthropology, the study of the culture of people and the sub-cultures involved intrigues me.

However, the bottom line was I needed money and I wanted a job that I could do and leave, a work-shift without a lot of responsibility. For the record, I underestimated the job's responsibility. First, meet and greet, lots of details, the phone calls, and being alert for the family and the elders in the building. Receptionists are super key players in an organization and a good receptionist is worth their weight in gold. The best part of my job was the family aspect. The residents and the staff were family. We cherished our connections. The residents had an educational program set up to help employees advance their education. I took advantage of their generous offer and received a Certification in Gerontology from the University of Washington. They helped me, and I learned how to be more of service to them.

After about a year of my working the front desk, the residents told me they wanted to learn to drum. The activity director discussed the idea and we decided to start a drumming circle for elders. While we were talking about it, she said, now if I only knew someone to teach a beginning watercolor class. Well, she did not know that I painted, and it felt like a higher power or spiritual setup, and the beginning watercolor class was started. Both of these classes and the residents helped me become a better person with their wisdom and my new focus in life. Yes, we had our moments but lots of love in that group. It was a really remarkable time of creativity. At the same time, I continued to develop my intuitive healing skills. People periodically came to me to have me send some energy to their sore head, shoulder or back. I still had my small business practice.

AH HA Moments

Getting back to the inner and outer life. Sometimes people will have chaotic events in their life, but it does not seem to affect them. They continue on with their life and appear to move forward. In my experience, there are two types. One that allows themselves to process their feelings, and to be gentle with themselves, giving themselves some time to heal. The second group powered through the event with lots of activity. Sometimes, the *lots of activity* is because they really are that busy, and do not have time to process. A video I watched showed a woman with the disease of Alzheimer reliving a tragic event. He toddler son had opened the front door and then he ran into the street. She was at the door when she saw her child hit by a car. She had other children and a husband to take care of, and certainly not a lot of time to process her own grief. She had to be there for her family. Her mind went back to that day and she kept reliving it. I was taught in my Alzheimer disease training that if you talk or process with the person about a particular painful memory, it will help them resolve the memory.

Peace on Earth

PEACCIOR

Once I was in a circle gathering with a group of people. As we participated in a ceremony I heard through clairaudience, psychic hearing the word Peaccior. A Peaccior's focus, intent and action are one of peace and love. The opposite of warrior. Another participant said the word in the circle and confirmed what I had heard. I later went to the dictionary and found no such word existed. The word was peacemaker. However, peace*maker* is not the embodiment of love. Rather it is the action step of love. Peaccior is more visceral and thus more powerful of a concept. Just like warriors are trained to do battle, Peacciors can be trained to do peaceful love.

Part of my peace healing work has been to send certain sacred rocks to different areas. Here are some of my stories. First, I always pray holding the sacred rock for pure intention of good. Next, I send healing energy vibration to the rock. For me this work is sacred and divinely inspired.

One day in meditation I had a knowing, that is, a strong thought, to give one or two rocks to someone to take to Northern Ireland. I knew two lads that I had met at one of the local Irish pubs, but I didn't know them very well. The tavern often held Irish music sessions where I sat in with my bodhran. These two men mentioned to me they were going home to Northern Ireland. Well, immediately I knew I was to give a rock or rocks to these guys. However, I was scared to talk to them, big time! I had the rocks in my pocket and was worried what I was going to say. So, I approached them fully expecting to call me crazy. They listened to my request. A softness came over one of the men and then a smile. He was pleased to do it. Happy to be of service. I gave him and his friend I think two rocks. A few weeks later, they had returned from their trip home. They sought me out and wanted to give me a full report. They had taken the rocks to Northern Ireland and had buried them per my request. They told me where they buried them but

I have forgotten. The rocks were loaded with prayers and good intentions for the peace process in Northern Ireland. We both had done our part and mostly we never talked much after that. It taught me not to underestimate the power of divine intentions.

Once again, I had a knowing that a rock or rocks were needed in Paris. One of my clients, Sandie, was traveling to Paris. This was her first trip and she excited to go. She was very pleased to take the rock with her. When I contacted her recently to remind me of the story, she told me she has told the story many times. The rock I gave her was full of prayers for Paris. She had asked me where she should place the rock. I told her that she would know. She trusted this was true. She was very mindful of keeping track of the rock. She kept it in a small pocket in her jean. It had arrived safe to Paris. As she was going to take the rock out she noticed the smallish rock had broken into three pieces. She decided to put the pieces in three different areas. Two she threw in a subway station. The last one she placed in Monceau Park by a huge tree. This park was close to a school, and it felt right to her that this was a good place for the last bit of rock. When she returned home, she mentioned the part about the rock breaking into three pieces. I looked surprised. I told her that I had originally thought I was going to give her three rocks but instead one seemed to be the right choice.

My third sacred rock story involved my friend Kathleen traveling to Palestine, Jordan and Israel. Again, I received during meditation a knowing to give her a rock to take and bury. When I approached her, she was very glad to do the work. At first, I thought she would take only one rock. However, as the time for us to meet neared I realized she was supposed to take three rocks. One went to Jerusalem near the sacred space for all religions and one went to Jordan. The last rock returned home. I had thought it might go to Syria, but it did not. It is on my altar now. Kathleen told me she had been in a café full of Syrians in Jordan but did not have a strong feeling to give the rock to anyone. Language was a barrier for communication. We were both happy to have the sacred rocks in place to help heal the land. Healing the land can affect the people in a loving way.

AH HA Moments

The earth is more loving and wiser than I knew. YEAH!   Double YEAH!   Triple YEAH!

Women's Psychic Energy

Often women especially women during their menses, do not sit with men in ceremony because of their powerful psychic connection of blood and life force. Men knew they had less energetic ability, women knew it was an honor to be separate to do their own divine work. Men needed to be together for their own spiritual lives. An example would be if you had an opera star singing in the local choir, that opera star's ability could and probably would overwhelm the vocals of the choir. It might be distracting for some of the choral and the audience. The women are the spiritual, energetic rock stars of a gathering, but men's energy is the lightning rod to get things moving. They have the natural ability to focus on moving the group spiritual energy to the altar or center.

It is possible maybe even plausible that these words lead some readers to view this as a separation of the sexes. This is not my intention. The lightning rod is very important to help direct the force of nature to a particular focus. Rather, the participation of *teamwork love* blesses men and women. Teamwork can include the animals, the plants and all of nature. We are social beings, includes most creatures, fish even swim in schools.

The Universe Loves Me

I am an artist and I have a studio at a city-owned building. Recently during one of my Open Art Studio events, a young man stopped by to see my art work. I was feeling a little overwhelmed with the crowd and wanted some nurturing. He smiled and said, "This card is for you and this message is for you." The card that he gave me said, "The Universe

Has a Message for you, I Loves You." How is that for an uplift? I just love the way the universe embraces me. This time I cried a few emotional tears of wow-ness— because art openings are often nerve-wracking and I put a lot of pressure on myself. Good old universe reminding me of my true essence of spirit and how much I am loved.

Here is another lovely confirmation that the universe has my back. I wrote a check to a photographer friend of mine and knew I needed to move some money over to my checking account. However, I was also processing some old memories and in grief mode. This is an old pattern for me. The way I have solved the problem in the past is by connecting my checking with my savings for overdraft protection. Well, the check went through and I had the exact amount, down to the same number of needed cents, in my checking account. My balance was at 0. This time *I* moved the money between accounts not the bank. It was empowering and I felt so watched over and taken care of. Many of us have our own stories about being lucky or feeling blessed by something that happened.

AH HA Moments

What if the inner and outer matched? What if all that cultural training to mold us to being perfect people and culturally acceptable was just teaching self-hatred? Do babies have the capability to feel self-hatred about themselves and their behaviors? Or are they in a connected state of being with self? When babies are uncomfortable, gassy stomach, a wet diaper, or hunger, they let us know. We would be shocked to find out that they monitor their thoughts about their physical sensations to please other people. When does, this monitoring begin? Does it matter? Rather when does this behavior stop? Some will say that the development of the frontal cortex of the brain allows for abstract reasoning to begin. It also can be argued it can create the intellectual ability to be manipulated by guilt and shame. Neither of these are true emotions because they have to go through the frontal cortex of the mind to be felt. What are true emotions? Emotions that are visceral response, such as joy, anger, fear, happiness, and sorrow. Think about a baby and their simple emotional response to life. True fear is a baby hearing a loud noise, being scared and crying for comfort. Fear is an also a direct result of overthinking. For instance, a friend was supposed to call and had ignored your two emails. You wonder if they are upset with you or if they are okay. Later you learn they forgot and had been away from their electronics. Lots of thinking, what if's? Worry without knowledge is a brain in knots. Most, if not all of us, have been there, and then kick ourselves again for all the time wasted thinking. Will we do it again? Yes, most likely. Mindful meditation training will help us recognize it and redirect the thoughts.

The Beginning: Earth-Sky Connect

First Ceremony

This is my process. When I am intuitively listening, I get a knowing as to what area of the earth needs some healing work. The outcome can be different. I have been doing earth-sky energy work for almost 30 years. A friend of mine about thirty years ago invited three women including myself to come and bring energy to the earth from the sky. It was a sacred ceremony and she informed us she was a Celtic Druid priestess from the sacred Druid world. Someone had gifted me with a large crystal with masculine energy. It was shaped as a penis and two testicles. I bought it with me because I felt it was the right action.

Looking back, I realized that hidden piece of public land had a vortex. At the time, I could feel it had been used in the past for sacred ceremonies. This was the first time I begun to understand the significance of the connection with the earth-sky action. I was honored to be a participant. The ceremonial leader with a woman trained in Druid and

Native American ceremonial techniques. During the ceremony, she initiated our small group into the Druid priesthood. As I remember she learned these techniques from family members. The other two women initiated into the sacred circle appreciated this ceremony as much as I did. This was a special sacred opportunity for us to be present with the earth and sky. She explained how to draw the energy down to the earth, and used my crystal, as a wand to pinpoint positive loving energy from the sky to the center of the circle. She talked about the ancient oak trees and their significance in the Celtic sacred tradition. She touched our heads and said some sacred words. We all felt so blessed after the ceremony and had a picnic to share food with each other. It was the beginning of my work with the earth and the universe. Today I do not remember the exact words of the ceremony nor the exact location. It was a hidden grassy spot on a hill overlooking Lake Washington. The grove was hidden from the street by bushes and trees. The high priestess felt this had been a sacred spot for the Native American people who had lived in the area.

She felt the sacred circle had been honored and use in the past for ceremonies. It occurred to me that she had been directed by her spirit guides to this place. When we first entered the area, the sun was shining and indeed it had the feel of light and love. All of us benefited from her awareness, and reveled in the magic of the land.

Focus on the Positive

I was in Latvia during the end of Russian occupation, and the people of Riga all came out in their traditional garments, and sang their country's folk songs. The energy was lovingly amazing. I wondered if you could take that energy floating up and away from the city, and send it to another part of the world for healing purposes. It made sense to try and I sent it to Seattle, since I would be home in a few days. When I returned home, the energy was not there. I was disappointed, the experiment did not work, but, oh well, I tried. The next day the light bright joyful energy showed up. It took longer to get to Seattle than it did for me to go home. Nevertheless, it worked. Ever since, when there is a similar event, for instance, when my beloved Seahawks won the Super Bowl and downtown was full of loving, celebratory, joyous people, I have gathered the energy and directed it to a war zone in the Middle East.

AH HA Moments

A lot of my life is internal creative connection. My world is now in the void of being. Later I review my own choices. I appreciate the beauty of being a creative soul.

Earth Energies: The Ley Lines

I had the good fortune to meet someone who studied ley lines and knew quite a bit about them. She and her husband had a background in earth sciences. To her the ley lines were a given. She asked me if I had ever noticed how often churches would be on the same street for miles. She theorized church members instinctively recognized a healing light energy flow or line. She also showed me a photo of sheep or cows laying all in a single row. A bit odd that they did not want to enjoy the full green pasture. She said animals can feel the lighter energetic difference. I had to agree with her based on the photos. Plus, I had noticed how churches are often on the same street. Ley lines have been described as the acupuncture path of the earth. Based on my own ability to read energy, I agree with this interpretation. Others most likely know where the acupuncture points are located. I have not studied this. To add to my thoughts on the subject I googled Ley Lines. I was surprised it was considered potentially mythical, and that the geographic aspect of the lines focused on different sites rather than the grid aspect of the ley lines. Also, it is unclear to me if people realize that the ley lines are not flat on the earth's surface but extend upward to the atmosphere boundary, and downward in the earth. It has occurred to me to help keep our earth in tiptop shape we must pay attention to these ley lines. This is a great research topic for some scientist. With all our measuring tools, surely, we can now track this geographic phenomenon.

The Earth Is Our Ally

The earth has been a shelter from the storm for so many of us. When we are full of emotion we go to the earth, much like a good mother, to be comforted. Sometimes like a child we run to the earth to feel her warmth beneath our bodies. I say warmth, but in winter her gift can be the cold. Yes, it is cold, but it is so invigorating, and it pushes a person to keep moving their body. Both scenarios offer a connective interaction with being alive. That connectedness continues with a garden. How many of us plant a flower in the Spring? How many of us pull a weed? On the other hand, how many feel out of sorts after we garden. We may feel sore but gardening is not prone to give people nightmares. It is prone to give people a good night's sleep.

Do you not have a garden and kill all your houseplants? Here is another idea for an earth-sky connection. Go outside, and go for a walk on a path, feel the earth under your feet. I particularly like walking in the mud. It is a little slippery, cushiony, and the challenge is to keep your socks and pants dry.

One of the lessons I learned in my energetic studies was to go to the earth, talk to the earth, and bury your painful emotions. The earth is our mother and will transmute this. Through my own work, I believe Mother Earth has changed, and can no longer accept these dense heavy emotions.

Where do, these emotions go if we want to transmute them? Well, I have found in my energy work that it is very effective to gather the dense emotions, such as hate, and rage; contain them in a pink bubble. Visualize this pink, sturdy bubble going up into space towards a black hole. This is what the black hole is designed to do, to absorb matter and change the matter into nothingness. The discovery of black holes came at a time when we urgently began to need them.

AH HA Moments

The earth is part of the universe. Sometimes I forget.

Vortex Strategies for the Planet

Vortex funnels are great ways to transport energy from the planet to outer space. It is also a great way to transport energy from outer space to the earth. I wrote about my first introduction to earth-sky energy earlier in the book. It felt this had been a sacred spot for the Native American people who had lived in the area. What I did not realize until years later that a sacred vortex was there. When we first entered the area, the sun was shining, and indeed it had the feel of light and love, much like certain vortexes I have since encountered or cocreated.

I also have created two healing vortexes in the Seattle area. One is on Whidbey Island at a Nature Conserve, and the second one is in Discovery Park. One of my friends who is a mindful meditator teacher and reads energy, was eager to tell me about them. She wanted to know if I knew about them. I have to admit it was with some mischievous smugness that I acknowledged I had cocreated with earth/sky to make them. It was a nice confirmation for me that people were benefiting from them.

Vortex: Evil Troubles

Once a client asked me to go to their home. Her son had developed drug problems and mental illness. At times, he was delusional. He had become violent, the violence escalated and he killed someone. He was arrested and tried for murder. He was sentenced to prison and was housed in the mental health ward. She asked me if I would go to her home and see if I could sense anything about her son's bedroom. She always wondered if the room was haunted or something. Her house for the most part was fine. I did not detect any major energy problems. She ushered me to her son's room. YES, indeed there was a problem with the room. Near the closet, or in the closet, I sensed that there was a transport funnel for dead people's spirits. This was not just any people; these people had died evil and been sent to their next destination, hell? Or another planet or whatever. It was going to outer space, but was that the final destination. It was full of activity, think highway, full but not crowded. One after another flew up this energetic tube. My client asked me would her son be influenced by this energetic hose. Very possibly, I said not all spirits want to go to the next path level. They want to stay back and continue their wicked human lives. Often, they are looking for unprotected bodies to enter. This type of interaction is called walk-ins. An apt name for a spirit that just walks in to a person's body.

I know from personal experience what it feels like to have a walk-in within my body. A number of walk-in spirits entered my body as a child, and affected my relationship with my sister. I talk about this later in the book.

Flying dreams can happen when a person is asleep, and leaves their body for an out of body experience. People remember flying and often are having an out of body experience. This is not dangerous but if you are in a room with wandering spirits without a proper sense of a good boundaries, you are in danger. An additional danger is having your head when you are sleeping facing in an eastern direction. Spirits find it easier to end from the east. This can also happen when people are under the influence of drugs or alcohol. I have seen it happen when someone is pronounced dead and somehow revives. Only this time the person no longer seems like themselves, sometimes to the extent they were a man and now act like a teenager. Oops, I am a little off topic.

So, the question was could this energetic pathway of evil be removed? Her son was now gone but it made her feel better about the situation. She wanted it cleared. She knew she would eventually sell her home, and did not want another homeowner to ever experience living through this type of pain, and living grief. What to do to clear this menacing vacuum pathway of evil. I became quiet and meditated on the problem. Some people might call it an issue, but if you had an evil energetic highway coming through your home, it is a gigantic problem!

During meditation, my vibration lightened, and I understood this energetic funnel was really a vortex of energy and was a transport vortex. After thinking about it, I decided the safest solution was to seal it. Years later—yesterday, in fact—I went by the house. I wondered if the transport vortex had returned. No, the energy was still light and fluffy. I had placed a small vortex in the area to keep the energy from getting stuck in muck and it worked. Glad the next owner could live in a peaceful setting. I had never tried to seal a vortex but I knew it was possible. After I sealed it, the vortex collapsed, and a few spirits were stranded in the sealing. I was able to visualize a mini-spaceship of light to send them to their next destination. This spaceship was placed in a pink bubble of love and sent to the universe. I do not remember if I visualized them going to a black hole, or their next best destination of light. This extra boundary of love and light insured that these spirit people were not available to roam the earth as walk-ins. Pink bubbles are very strong and hold a higher vibration that these evil inhabitants.

Since one bubble was full I made another large pink one. I talked to the creepy people and they were not cranky or rude to me just curious as to what was happening to them. I tried to explain it the best I could. One did not want to go into the pink bubble but I used the guiding force of white light and he went into the bubble. My next concern was, how far did the energy tube go. We went to the basement and I could see that my visual intention thoughts of sealing it had closed it beneath the home. Next I redirected the energy to outside for a quick minute. I wanted to make sure any heavy energy was no longer underneath this house. No one wants a septic tank full of old shit under their home. I went down hundreds of feet and cleared the energy. During the meditation, the vortex's duties were complete and did not need to be changed to another geographical area. My client felt that the energy had shifted and was grateful. In a couple years, she did sell her home, letting go of the past and welcoming the new.

Focus on the Path of Light

Receiving the message to stay in the lightness of joy, as time passed I felt more and more that I was transitioning to work in the light using the state of glee and bliss. My early experience had been working with the darker side of emotions, but during prayer and meditation, I felt guided to move into working with the light. Personally, I was torn by this idea. I felt that many people could benefit from healing their darker emotions. I told myself I was a talented facilitator in helping people. A person could say I was lukewarm in my acceptance of my new path. Or, they could say I was resistant to the change of giving up my hero's cloak. One step forward, two steps back. Thinking and Doing are two different energies. I have had to learn my lesson the hard way, more than once, but life is a process not a destination. I also now recognize love and happiness are great ways to heal the earth. And why not, be part of that team?

The African Medicine Man

One time an Irish friend told me about Shea Butter. An African friend of hers was selling it. He had given her a sample. She had been using it and it really helped her dry skin. She thought as a massage therapist I could use the product. Certainly, I am open to different products especially for dry skin. She gave me his phone number and I called him to set a time to discuss his product. We met at a little coffee shop downtown or on Capitol Hill. I remember it had lots of light through the café windows. He gave me a small sample of the product. It was high quality, a thick paste. However, the quantity volume for a wholesale price was more than I could use. As we talked I sensed he was much more than a business man selling a product. I sensed he was medicine man and he knew a lot about the art of healing energy and herbs.

Also, it felt to me he came from a family of traditional healers. At first, he denied it. I told him I saw his energy so I knew he had this ability as did some of his ancestors. After the initial, what are you talking about, he shifted. It was as if a light switch was turned on. His energy became brighter, and bigger. He looked around, it appeared to judge his audience and if anyone was paying attention to us. He started talking about the Nigerian Chewing Stick (Fagara zanthoxyloides) and pulled out a bag of these twigs and gave it me. He said it was good for cleaning the teeth and a treatment of a toothache. I believe he said it had properties to kill germs, antimicrobial alkaloids. He started sharing his love of nature and the earth. He told me in his country, he was originally from Nigeria, there is a saying about plants helping with healing. He said he was taught to pray. One of the prayers was for the correct plant to help an ailing person. In his medicine way, he was taught that if you go into the forest, the needed plant would be found. These words had a profound effect on my experience with the plants. The idea he gave me was that the plants are there to help us heal. This was not a human being seeing the plants as something to use. Rather this was a human person cocreating with plants to help someone. How beautiful for me to think about plants sharing their energetic life force and knowledge with us, and for us. Yes, I do talk to my plants and I can feel that they appreciate being acknowledged. Sometime when I am in the woods I feel a branch reach out to me as if to say hello. It feels friendly and not a jarring poke. When I am in nature it is much easier for me to feel calm and meditative, although sometimes the elevation level gets me thinking about how much further it is to the top view.

Sky Connection

Much like the earth I do have connections with the sky and the air elements, such as a wind's direction and the air's precipitation. This one has been the most difficult for me to accept as a normal gift. The movie *Frozen* allowed me to get in touch with some of my own fears. Once again, my focus is on the asking, and not controlling the outcome. It really has to be for the highest good, such as improving the drought conditions in California.

AH HA Moments

> The earth loves to cocreate with us, but was
> not created for us.

Earthquakes

Earthquake Ponderings

What is the purpose of Earthquakes? We know what causes earthquakes from a scientific point of view. We understand seismic readings; we understand fault zones and some of us know what it feels like to be in an earthquake. The first earthquake I experienced was when I was in grade school. I had a slow trying-to-get-ready morning and everyone had already left for school and work. I was walking up the street, about a third of a block along. All of a sudden, the ground began to move and I looked up to see my neighbor's two story home moving, much like a ship in rough waters. It was an amazing sight. I thought *earthquake* and remembered during earthquakes you are supposed to be under something. I also remembered photos in *Life* Magazine about the Alaska earthquake with large deep gaping splits and holes in a street where the earth separated. I worried that the earth would open up and swallow me. I raced to my neighbor's house, the nearest structure. As I was running towards the building I slipped on the grassy incline and fell on my bottom. Just as quickly as it started it was over. I continued my walk to school because I did not want to be any later than I was. When I got to school everyone was still in the indoor play area. I think the principal was trying to decide about the school day. A little while later it was decided it was safe, the earthquake had stopped. We went to our classrooms. I felt very lucky that I was not marked tardy.

Yes, I have worked with the earth and earthquakes. It is definitely a cocreative process with the earth, the land and the movement. Earthquakes are a way for the earth to shake off or clear energy that has become stagnant. An important distinction to know: I cocreate with the earth rather than control or demand an outcome. It is vital to let go of the attachment to outcome and focus on the action of love.

Nepal: 2015 Earthquake

After months of receiving a clear message in meditation that I needed to slow down and become quiet, I did not. My immediate thought was: I am too busy, much too busy. What happened next is a classic Anne Marie story. I fell and broke my foot. This requires rest. During the next meditation, I swear I heard, "Are you too busy now?" So, I guess my guides have a sense of humor. Lying on my sofa with my foot up I had lots of time to meditate. I was also slightly bored. I wanted something to do. It was about that time that the severe Nepal Earthquake hit. It occurred to me that I could help. I wanted to make sure it was not my hero-ego and really came from a place of knowing. I meditated and knew my intention was for the best and highest good. How to help? I remembered an acquaintance I knew and she lived in Nepal. I decided to email her to learn if she was interested in cocreating with me, and being my detail person on the ground. The first is my journal entry and later my message correspondence with her. This is a way to show potential earth energetic workers my process.

May 11, 2015 (my journal entry)

Today I had a knowing that I was called to help clear the energy in Nepal. Another earthquake, this one 7.1, more people and buildings damaged, lives lost. I did some remote viewing and checked out the earth. The land mass was very rigid. It looked like cement instead of the earth's dirt. Oh, yes, I remembered that Mount Everest is the place to go for climbing a mountain. Having been at a mountain climber's funeral once, that attracted many mountain climbers and male dominant energy was so present in the room. At that time, I realized that people climbed Mount Everest not to honor her but to conquer the mountain. It became apparent that Nepal and Mount Everest were very patriarchal and dominated the female population. This domination was also apparent in their own blocking of the female energy of themselves. This model is no longer serving a useful purpose on this earth. The earth in her wisdom is clearing these cultural ideologies through earthquakes and other means. I googled the problem and found an explanation of what is happening now. The tectonic plate form India is bumping up to the plate in Nepal. However, Nepal plate is rigid and allows no give. The result is earthquakes. They predict the earthquakes will continue and believe a larger earthquake is possible and even probably. MMM

Just found this.
http://www.newsweek.com/nepal-earthquake-could-have-been-manmade-disaster-climate-change-brings-326017.html

Email to my friend in Nepal:

Hi, we met in Seattle at an art event. Did I mention I do energetic work for the earth? Earth-sky connection. I am glad we met so my message may not seem so odd. Last night in prayer and meditation I received a knowing that it is time for me to help. As you must know your art work is even more important than I realized when we met. I knew it was sacred female work but did not really understand. I admire you even more now! Your art is very important for the needed change for women's power and status in your society. Why am I saying this because last night I went into energetic exploratory mode of the area? The area has too much male energy and needs to be balance with female energy. Your area has strong dominant male warrior energy. When I did a remote viewing of the situation I saw only stuck energy like dried cement throughout the huge area. I am visualizing going very deep into the earth when your area was more male/female balanced and am slowing bringing the energy up from the earth. I also send energy from other global areas that honor female energy. One of the places is The Aztec temple of the moon outside Mexico City, some sacred wells in Ireland and one place in Russia. I am on my iPhone but I will write more later. At this point it is better if this is a private conversation between us because it is in the early stage of creative development and fragile. Know the earth is really your friend and wants the best for everyone. Love and Big Hug!

Reply from the friend:

Great to hear from you Anne Marie in the midst of devastating situation. Definitely we need more energy...

My reply to her:

I have some energetic systems running now, and will continue to clear the rigid stuck energy. Are there any female sacred temples or wells in Nepal or nearby? And if available could you send me their names and location. When it is time to include it, I can easily access the information. Thank you! As much as I hate to think of you in this unsafe earthquake zone, your understanding of female sacred energy is much needed now.

May 14, 2015: email from the friend in Nepal:

Guheshoari temple is one I can think of ... in Kathmandu, nearby pashupari temple... Google it for the exact location other one is living goddess, basantapur, Kathmandu, where most of the temple destroyed but living goddess and her place is not damaged at all...

My reply:

Excellent! Perfect timing. Just finished doing some energy balancing on Mt Everest. Realized Mt Everest need to be honored for her own beautiful being of earth not to be something to be conquered. Working on restoring the awareness of her truth of greatness. It is in process now. Now I can really appreciate the deep tragedy of Nepal but I did laugh when you told me about the living goddess temple not damaged at all. Confirmation of what we both already know. Love and Big Hug to you, your family and the people of Nepal.

My friend sent me a link:

http://news.nationalgeographic.com/2015/05/150514-nepal-earthquake-kathmandu-kumaris-newar-buddhism/

I replied:

Thanks for the article.!! It helps me understand more. Tomorrow I can write you and tell you more about what was done today. The two sacred women's temple were very helpful in my work today.

I replied again:

Where to start. First Mount Everest. I am directing the heavy toxic energy in the earth through Mount Everest to a black hole. I have been sending heavy dense emotions for years to cleanse the earth. Not sure which black hole but scientists have found one now with moisture. They had to change their ideas about black holes. As you know in Asian thinking water symbolizes emotions. So, it occurred to me that particular black hole might be the one I use. Anyway, after directing the toxic energy away from the earth to a black hole for cleansing I started the process of bringing the universe's energy pure love to earth. The best place to setup an energy vortex yesterday (thank you) think the size of a pinhead, is in the female goddess shrines. I have expanded the small energy vortex think of a rope or cable from the sky to the earth. It is about 3 inches in diameter as of this morning. Placing pure love into the earth. Pure love does not have a dualistic form it is formless.

FYI the earth's vibration is 18th dimension and the universe is 21st Dimension. This is according to scientists, one from Harvard.

Emails from me to my friend:

I also read about the earthquake in Bharatpur and found a Kali shrine so included that this morning. Years ago, did one or two paintings of mountain peaks being women's breast. If I find the picture in my art studio I will send you a photo. Photo is available on website.

***

So, this has been an elaborate plan to clear the energy for Nepal. I do think that everything is now in place to continue to healing.

***

It is moving slowly. 50 miles daily. So tonight, it will be at 100 and tomorrow 50 until it feels like it needs to be slowed down even more. I am so curious as to how this will affect the psyche mind of the people of Nepal. The women and some men are so ready for a change. This is all part of the needed clearing for the earth.

My friend replies:

I'd like a little more clarification, just so I'm on the same page with you and can help you. Here's what I understood... Your truth and true work is Earth-sky Connection. Could you tell me more about this? Are you saying this is what you do, as in the name of the service you offer? Or are you saying this is how you do it, as in the process of what you do? Or is this your message, the big thing you want people to know and get out of

working with you? Or something else?
(Apologies for not getting it off the
bat. :^))

I replied to her:

So, the short answer to your
question is I look at the problem of the
earth situation, listen to guidance, and
also use my tool bag to figure out the
best gentle way to clear the energy of
the earth. Recently a person that does
energetics wanted to understand what
vortexes are and wondered if she made
them too. We went to a local Seattle
Park that had been an unofficial
homeless site until the city fenced it
off, and I cleared the energy and she
witnessed it. I clear the energy because
of my tool bag, love, God and my
vibration. What I did was find a good
spot of heavy energy and make a
vortex to clear out the toxicity. At that
time, I ask how far to go down to pull

the energy out. I get the answer think that distance and make a vortex, similar to a cyclone funnel. My friend was more than surprised by the energy of the vortex, than she was how I travel to timelessness, move the energy a year ahead until all the heavy energy is gone, and return it to the present. I seal the vortex and remove it. I might leave a small hose of universal loving energy to maintain the higher vibration of the land. This particular event was probably a five-mile radius... When we returned to her car it was obvious the street energy was light and peaceful. She was impressed :^) and understood why this ability is sacred and not an energetic show and tell event. A person could hurt themselves without the proper vibration of love. And I bet you all will get that. Each case is different. However, I know that it is now much more beneficial for me to share my story and to think about their own energetic contributions to the earth and to each other.

Her reply:

I'd like a little more clarification, just so I'm on the same page with you and can help you.

My explanation:

What do I do? I turn into the land the same way I can turn into people. I do not like to know a lot at first. I like to just feel the energy. If there has been some trauma I can feel it and it is a relatively easy clean up. I go down so many feet and take the heavy energy out of the earth into the sky. I got the idea of sending heavy energy to black holes because of how they function—- no garbage in space. I started working with vortexes years ago as a way to transport heavy energies from the earth. I usually use an energetic hose to bring the energy from the universe. It is a higher vibration and it allows for a gentler infusion of higher vibration energy. Each case is different. I was at this energetic conference about 15 years ago and a woman stared at me and said," Who are you?" I told my name and she said, "No, who are you?" She was the first person that could see my Earth-Sky Connection. I remembered immediately crying because she was the first person that recognized me. Obviously, I never talked about my abilities because I was afraid of what people would think. Plus, I was modest and did not realize my talent. People said we had the same energetic abilities and I believed them. I was confused when they did not know what I was talking about. And accused me of making it up. That was then and now I have a better understanding of me.

She stopped communicating with me. A clear example of it is all about me and not the cocreating process. Learn from my mistakes.

AH HA Moments

Thinking and being are two different experiences. Thinking does not always lend itself to being in the moment. When our thoughts are connected with our breath, our bodies, and our intuition it is easier to sort out the difference between a thought and suppressed feeling. When we become quiet from within, but not necessarily thought-free, we allow our being to tell us," What is going on?" Breathe in the thought, connect the breath to your body, focus on your heart and stay with the feelings of the heart. Breathe these feelings and stay with them. Emotions are not bottomless holes, however painful. If you allow them to be felt, the mind will lighten with love.

Clearing Homes and Home Sites

First Property Clearing

Many years ago, a friend I had worked with at juvenile court told me about her property problem. She and her husband had recently bought a house with some acreage. They were both thrilled as each had grown up in rural areas and part of the property had a lovely creek with gentle sounds of rushing water. She had some concern about a particular area near the creek. It did not feel right to her. She asked me if I would check it out. She was right. It felt as if some sexual violence had occurred. The land still carried the trauma of the event. I confirmed with her that indeed her instincts were correct, and told her what my intuitive feeling was. I cleared the heavy energy and sent it on it way off the earth to the sky. Until recently it has been floating around the universe. Or, at least as I write this, I checked in with the remembered energy. It was indeed floating in space. I had not learned the black hole technique when I first started. Since time is fluid, I was able to move that block of heavy energy to a black hole. The atmosphere does not need to be our dumpster. Back to the story, after the clearing we both felt a significant change in the area. She reported no further problems.

The Sacred Ceremony for a Home

Once I was asked to have a ceremony for the land of a client. Her plan was to have a few cherished friends and herself to help purify and bless the land. We had a bonfire and our chairs were around the bonfire. Each of the people contributed something. Unfortunately, I do not remember all the details. This is what I do remember. First I got lost trying to find her home. She had to come and get me and I followed her back to her home. Second, people were drinking alcohol and I had neglected to tell the host it was important to do this ceremony with a minimum of alcohol. I had sent very few instructions as to how to prepare for this ceremony because I figured everyone knows. Why I thought that, who knows? I do not think that anymore.

The owner of the property introduced me and the guests, and I had a pleasant interchange of small talk. I realized that these were dear friends of the owner of the property, loved her deeply, and wanted to support her in her request. However, they had never participated in this type of land ceremony. I hoped it was not too jaw-dropping for them. I had brought some rocks. The owner had a degree in geology and she loved them as much as I did. The rocks were set to show a border for the sacred circle. First, I drummed and called in the four directions. I next called the wind and the wind came up. The trees' leaves rustled in the wind as if to say, we are here and ready to witness. I remember calling in the birds and birds came and began to sing, we did a small circle dance and everyone participated and wanted to participate. Afterwards we toasted marshmallows in the sacred fire to give us some food to share with the emphasis on play. The participants enjoyed themselves and were very happy to have witnessed nature as a willing participant too—for the love of their friend. To be honest I was surprised as well.

This was the first time I led a circle of people who had no prior experience with sacred ceremony. I was very glad the wind and the birds came on their cue. A person can ask, but that does not mean the wind or the birds will come. Free Will Choice is always there for all of us.

Energy Trolls

Two decades ago, a friend told me that their land was problematic and they did not know why. They had smudged the house but it still felt weird. Could I come over and investigate the problem? When I went to their lovely home with a beautiful view of the sea and Mount Rainier, I was struck by the beauty of the architecture and the expansive area of land. However, my friend was right. It did have a heavy creepy energy to the land, particularly one area near the garage or the original small house. As I began to investigate the problem, I began to meditate to raise my vibration to see the problem area. In order to clear this problem, the vibration of the land need to be transformed to a lighter less dense energy. I began to raise the vibration of the land through intention. The land began to clear and the heavy energy was being directed through an invisible funnel to a black hole in the universe. All of a sudden, I sensed something else was happening. In my mind's eye, I saw this massive creature, a giant tumbleweed furry creature. It had eyes, hands and legs, mostly it was a big ball of something. At that time, I thought of it as a troll from the dark side of evil, a relative of the troll from the Norwegian fairy tale, *Three Billy Goat Gruff.* The troll on this property needed heavy, dark emotional energy to stay comfortable. He also preyed on people's thoughts, and had the ability to influence moods and sweep their angry, fearful thoughts into his own dank body as fuel. It was hard for the residents and their visitors to stay happy when this troll inhabited the space beneath the property. The creature was upset because all of the heavy energy, his feeding source, was disappearing. He needed this energy to continue to survive. He wanted me to stop and was quite fierce, moving towards me. I immediately placed him in a bubble wrap of white light, an energetic cage, as it were. He was not able to move much, and so we began to communicate through telepathy. The creature was not happy and really wanted to stay there. However, the creature knew, with the heavy energy being sent to a black hole, that his food source was leaving. We talked about the next step. The next step could be going to a black hole with lots of heavy surrounding energy to use for fuel. The creature knew without a heavy dark energy source he would die, and if he was the only living troll his species would become extinct. He opted for a ride in a transporter to a black hole. I placed the creature in a transport vehicle of white and pink light and made a giant energy hose around him. He left, and went to outer space with the destination determined by the magnetic force of the black hole. Yes, there is a painting of one of these troll-like creatures.

Recently a client asked me to clear her property. She had tried to clear the property twice. Once, she hired someone and the second time, herself, knowledgeable about smudging and energetics tried. Both attempted failed. The heavy energy always returned, or else refused to dissipate.

By inadvertently viewing property of the wrong address, I understood what the problem was. I saw the same troll type I had seen in my minds-eye years ago. Only this time it was a family of trolls. Who knew that trolls could reproduce? These trolls were living near her house. I believe it was the house next door. Google Earth, usually very reliable for an address site had taken me to a different house. The good news is I was able to spot the trolls through my minds-eye viewing because I went to the wrong place. I had the correct address but for some reason the wrong link. Later, she gave me the correct address link, and I did another google search. As I mentioned earlier, trolls like to encourage fear and angry, dense emotional energy, because it is their food source. When her house was cleared, the trolls just transported back emotional heavy dense energy, to encourage the continuations of heavy dense emotions. Since it was a family of trolls they must have needed more to survive. Hence, they went to the neighbors' home for food. I set up a plan to remove the trolls. I enjoyed making those enticing transport vehicles to convince the trolls how enjoyable the ride would be. Since there were so many trolls not all of them wanted to ride in the same vehicle. The younger trolls liked the idea of little bumper cars. The adult trolls liked the idea of a space ship with comfortable seating. They were all going to the same place so they knew they would not being separated. Even trolls like a little adventurous choice in their lives. After I did the clearing the client started talking about how it was not the same piece of property. It felt so much better.

It occurred to me with so many trolls thriving nearby they had been pulling energy from a much larger geographical area. It may have helped other neighbors too. Only they will not know why they feel so much better. It does not matter; the outcome matters most. So, it appears my intuition and Google Earth directed me to the root problem source, if not the correct address. Can we say, Yeah! for intuition hunches, following them, and divine intervention? The actual property to be cleared had some pockets of problems, a previous burglary, a broken romance, and some stagnant energy, but nothing like the heavy dense energy of the trolls. The owner had said she had tried to clear the energy, but the heavy dense energy stuck around in the home. Of course, the trolls would have lent some of their energy to feed the lingering heavy emotions of anger, fear, and the act of aggression. With the trolls being safety transported to their next destination the space clearing had no interference, and the problem was solved. The home and property sold almost immediately.

Time to Sell the Family Home

One of my friends told me she and her husband had decided to sell their home. She was getting it market-ready, and suggested I do a Space Clearing for them. She said the energy always felt a little weird. As it turned out, it was a most interesting challenge. The house rested on some sort of energy pool. I saw in my third eye and at the time wondered if this was even possible. I called it a schist because it reminded me of an interior giant blister. Since I wanted more information, I called an acupuncturist, a friend of mine. I explained what I had seen in my vision. "Had she ever seen a trapped pool of energy in the body?" She said, "Yes, in acupuncture it is called a capillary pool." She said it was not like the blood capillaries, rather it was just a term used to describe the phenomenon. It occurred to me if the energy flowed in, it could flow out.

I told my friend about my theory. She corroborated my observation. She said about four years ago, the family remodeled the kitchen. The contractor told them that the house had not settled at all and had the original plumb line. He said that he had remodeled homes for years, and had never seen a house without some shifting. It was even more surprising because the house was over forty years old. He wondered, how was that even possible? Also, my friend said the outside plants grew much faster than their observed normal growth patterns. If a plant was supposed to grow four inches, the plant grew seven inches. No one knew why. We talked about the process and she added some more helpful details. Problem solving this was not a quick fix. I played with different ideas. A couple days later, I developed a safe gentle plan. Safety-first because if the energy pool was removed too quickly it might be harmful to the residents, including the family pet. My plan was to add small energy-carrying hoses going away from the energy pool. Slowly, the pool began to drain. It was also important not to create another energy pool somewhere else. So, the energy hoses were pointed in various directions to gently mix the energy flow back with the earth. Yes, this is all through vibrational intent. No reason to use real hoses.

Confirmation is always important when I do the work. The day before the house was scheduled to go on the market, I had my confirmation. One of the boards on the deck was slightly rotten. When someone placed their foot on the deck, the board broke, and his foot went down. No one was hurt, and the deck was quickly repaired. The energy was no longer a factor in holding up the structure. When the real estate agent wrote about the house to sell, he wrote, "This home has good karma. People feel it when they walk in the door. The house just feels good!" The owners never told him about the space clearing. Later, the new owners rave to my friend about how great the energy is in their new home. All confirmation of a change in the "something weird" previously noted in the house. I am glad. I do not know how common energy pools are or how they formed or why. A geophysicist might know. It is a fascinating phenomenon!

An Old Urban Building Clearing

An old urban building houses artist studios, a drafty dank basement, and lots of stories. The assignment was to clear the studios and the hidden dank storage areas. Let the fun begin. Before I arrived, I had begun to clear the area of the gallery. I had noticed problems a couple weeks earlier during the First Thursday Seattle Artwalk. Now as I entered I could feel the gentle light air in the gallery. The owner confided that things had been going better. He did not elaborate and I did not ask. First step was meeting the other artists and saying hello, and explaining my work. With that, we entered a door with a musky smell to it. It was cool, and dark. To my left was a large area with a skylight overhead. I could sense the despair, the misery and crowded conditions.

Now the area was almost empty, with assorted wood boards, concrete flooring and pipes. It felt as if two groups had lived there. One area, felt as if a group of Chinese immigrants had huddled together in this place. That energy had some fear and confusion, but it also felt like a team, it had a spirit of comradeship. It had a hint of hope and curiosity as to what the future will be. The next occupant group's energy had a huge sadness, disconnect and despair. It felt as if one person may have died there. Each person in this group seemed to feel isolated and might appear to others as withdrawn. Loneliness was the huge feeling that hung in the area.

I quickly went to work and begin to cocreate with the past, the building and memories. Each layer was acknowledged and cleared. When I had finished, we turned to our right and continued on towards the maze of boards. The area was dank, and dark. Apparently, people fell from the boards above, died, and workers just shoveled dirt over them as they added height to the ground. I felt five unrested souls; one was a woman. I placed them all in individual sacred bubbles of light, and requested they be sent to their next destination. The owner confirmed that he had heard people had fallen, died, and were buried there. He seemed surprised that there were only five. So, as a safeguard I set up an additional five transports so if some soul needed some help with their transition it was available.

Aside from the spirit/souls the most disturbing part was a heavy evil energy that also resided there. This energy felt like it had been in a body, possibly was a walk-in, but had a demon's spirit not a human spirit. To clear this energy, I prayed to God for protection, and called in the angels to protect and help me. Evil is never a match for goodness of love. The evil spirit was forced into a white light bubble, and sent to a black hole in outer space to be cleaned, and changed. The area immediately felt lighter and less scary.

We continued down the room, flashlight in hand, and continued to clear. One funny thing was the old water heater. Whoever brought that water heater into the building was not happy. Anger poured forth from the tub and the connecting pipes. It was almost comical. I bet no one told the installer how difficult the task was or maybe, he just had a really bad day. So, I removed the heavy energy. Most of us know that when we cook food the intention during the preparation is felt by the eaters. Food cooked with love tastes better.

Next was another area center but to the south of the area. This area also had a feeling of someone living there, but not so desperate, and a feeling of hopefulness and community. The owner said yes, some street kids had lived there before they were discovered. As I looked up I noticed the graffiti on the walls, it made the place feel more vibrant, someone wanted to dress the place up with color and art. Years ago, I worked with street kids and they may have had a tough life, but many were hopeful for their future self. They had just begun to test the waters of adulthood with its potential to live differently, than their parents. For some youth, living on the streets with a bonded-heart connection with other kids was much safer and less abusive than their own home.

There was an Ice Room which had had walls of fir wood. It had the best energy. The delivery iceman or men were happy folks. The ice room sang with joy. I was tempted to stay in that room, but that is not why I was there. The staircases had wear and you could feel the foot traffic of a yesteryear. I liked the feeling. It made me feel like I was part of kinetic history of stair walking.

At one time, there was a fancy bar in the area. As I stopped at a spot I asked the owner, "What was this?" Well, it turns out it most likely was where the patrons stood at the bar to get a drink from the bartender. This particular small area had flirty playful energy. Someone enjoyed themselves with a little harmless notion of romance. I decided to leave this energy in place. Why not, it has its own feel good vibe. The door and the stairs near the back of the basement had leftover energy from when bootleggers made the deliveries of booze. I did clear that energy. I felt a certain anxiety by the door with a sense the delivery man was looking for the police and hoping to slip in without being spotted. I did not feel any energy of anyone actually being caught and handcuffed. Rather, it was just the potential of being arrested.

Two of the artists had mentioned they had heard a ghost, and one had seen a ghost. The ghost was a young tall slim man dressed in a suit. His fashion apparel seemed to suggest a man living around 1910 or so. I saw him in my mind, and confirmed my own sighting with the one that had seen the ghost twice. The ghost definitely seemed benign and I offered to help him release his stuck stage. He appeared to be a little confused by the offer, and seemed to have mixed feelings about trusting me, but I think he decided to go.

Later the artists reported a sparkle in their studios and were enjoying their own productivity. During the next artwalk I went back to the building. For the most part the building felt good. However, there was a feeling in the hallway of a constricted throat, as if someone, a male, was having a panic attack. I noticed the energy was coming from the sub-basement area, an area I had only lightly cleared because it was not a usable space, and it did not seem necessary. The descending staircase was sealed by poured cement. No one was going to use it, and it was a holdover of the underground city of Seattle. Why did this happen? Most likely with the other energy now at a higher vibration that heavy dense energy in the sub-basement could not stay comfortable there. Was this a long dead spirit or feelings of trapped emotions that had been dormant in the sub-basement? At the time, I did not check the details of the cause. Use your intuition and trust your first response. Often that is the correct choice and dwelling on the details lowers the vibration.

The Hidden Lake

In Western Washington, we have a lot of underground streams and springs. Some of the land is clay-based. In Spring the underground water sources become more active, in the summer months they are more apt to dry up. Streams also disappear in the summer, and you can see a muddy path for the stream, or even a bare bone-dry path. One client asked me to clear her home and property. I sensed hidden water, and felt a deep reservoir or pond deep below the house at least 200-700 feet down depending on the season. The owner confirmed that indeed they had a water leakage problem in one room. In the winter a storm drain full of water gushes along to the sea and it is on the property. I became interested in the source of the water. The source of the water was a large field. Most likely the land at one time had a forest's root system to use the water. My sense is that the water without the trees has been building a reserve, an underground lake, for years. The underground stream to the sea was the only outlet for the lake. It occurred to me if I created, with permission from the earth and the water, small tributaries of water capillaries, to disperse the water to the surrounding areas, it would benefit the plants and thus the earth. Gentle but effective is my motto. Since the property uses a well it was important to be mindful to keep the well wet. As the water lessened, the damp heavy feeling of the home disappeared. Potential buyers had complained the house felt dark, which was really unbelievable since the house had lots of view windows, open sky spaces and plenty of light. My guess is it was their sense of the dank feel of the water. As you may remember or just know water is the symbol for emotions in Asian culture. Emotions can become stuck or heavy if contained. In this case, the containment was the pond beneath the house. After the clearing, the complaints of people about the darkness of the house stopped.

The Mystery to be Unraveled

A house has been on and off the market for years, at least seven or eight years. It was not selling. Yet it was a beautiful home with a lovely grand piano, lovely views of the water, and an expansive light feeling with high ceilings and plenty of windows. The kitchen was lovely with lots of potential for conversation and visiting. Upstairs a large open space was an ideal setting for a yoga/meditation room or an art studio. Yet the house had a sadness to it, parts of it felt lonely. Lonely, was it the property feeling lonely or the owners? First, I cleared the property and felt some connection with the owners. The house had a cord connecting it to somewhere in California. It seemed like it was the owners. One of the owners had mixed feelings about selling. The other issue was the house had a California feel, and it felt as if the house and the land never fully integrated as one unit.

The land did not feel valued by the owners and felt unseen. How that manifested in the property was part of the yard was on government property. Both the owners and the government office ignored this issue although it was in the disclosure real estate forms. Nothing was done by either party to remedy the situation, an outward sign of not being valued or integrated into the mix. As weeks passed the house did not sell and it still felt heavy. I saw a black hose attaching itself to the house and property. I followed it and it seemed to be connected with someone in California, but not the owners. Was it a previous owner or what? The energy had the feel of dark sorcery energy. I detached the cord from the house and it hung in the air trying to reattach itself to the house. I continued to gently detangle the cord, but it did not want to leave. So finally, I followed the cord energetically to California and returned it to its owner. It had female energy but all I could see was a female figure dressed in a long flowing dress with a hooded cape hiding her face. The house seemed free of the energy.

A few days later, I noticed that same energy had come back in full force. I asked the archangels to guard the house and four angels each positioned themselves at the corners of the property. Periodically I checked the house, and the menacing energy was still looking for an occasion to reattach itself to the home and property. I also felt the angels were doing battle with the despicable energetic warrior. So, something else was needed. I talked to the land and it wanted a higher vibration of love. With the blessing from the land I created two triangle funnels of the earth and sky. This funnel is a sacred site. The evil energy was no match for the love of the earth and the sky. This created a very special vibration for the house and for anyone that bought the house. People came to look at the home, but felt that it was not the home for them. They cited it was unique. Eventually after a few months on the market the home was sold. I do not know who bought the house, but I do know they have to have a certain vibration of light to live there. It is a Dali Lama kind of place now.

AH HA Moments

The earth is a loving, alive being. We are so lucky to have the earth guiding us to seek the light of living and to open our hearts in connection with animals and people. What if we are not the most intelligent soul-given creatures on earth? What if we are only the most destructive creatures on earth?

Simplicity, the Art of Living

What does that mean? Well, think about a big bowl of marbles, all different colors in the bowl. The mind becomes very active looking at all the colors in the bowl. If the mind is overactive, and engaged in naming all the colors (the thoughts), it is much harder for creative ideas and your intuition to interact with you. Sometimes keeping it simple allows for a more focused flow of knowing the next indicated steps. Remember, too much detail weighs down the energy. If you take all the marbles out of the bowl, the bowl weighs less and is lighter. If you replace it with the same number of marbles but all the same color it weighs the same but the mind is less engaged. This concept of simplicity in Feng Shui helps determine placement and the flow of the house. In the suggested reading section I have two books on the subject, one by Denise Linn, and the other by Nancy Santo Pietro.

A popular author today is Marie Kondo. She has written the book, *The Life-Changing Magic of Tidying up.* This book has become a global best seller. Her message is: de-clutter your home of cheerless belongings. Only keep items that bring you joy. Why? Because if you raise your home vibration it reflects back into your thoughts. This eventually made sense to me. I am a messy person and need all the reasons as to the why of decluttering. She is not saying live in scarcity in your home, rather, she is saying live in the joy of your home! You can have "stuff" just make sure you love the "stuff". Happiness and joy naturally raises a person's vibration. With the popularity of her book and system, it is lovely to witness how many people want to live in the simplicity of joy and happiness.

Mental Health vs. Paranormal

Mental health is not my area of expertise. Rather, this is what I have observed. Your experiences and ideas are valuable too and may be different than mine. This is my opinion.

People have asked me, is there a way to differentiate from delusional thinking and paranormal abilities. Yes, mental illness's delusional thinking has often but not always had a quality of dark negative thoughts, often a repetitive thought or story. As the person talks it feels more and more unbelievable. For instance, a person might talk about being mistreated in a work setting. It starts out believable enough. Someone might be talking about their job They talk about the stress of the job. They talk about a conflict with a fellow employee. The more they talk about the situation the more unbelievable it becomes. Their office is being monitored by hidden cameras. Some of the staff hate them. Someone at work is trying to poison them. Maybe, they believe their boss had placed cameras all through the person's home to monitor their actions. They cannot be convinced this is not true. They also have a tendency to ramble and talk and talk about their illusions. They exhibit high anxiety and are visually pained by their reality and want the listener to completely believe them.

Paranormally sensitive people usually are rather reluctant about talking about what they see or sense. They want to be sure that they are in a safe environment and people will not think they are crazy.

From my experience this fear is more a western European thinking process; most indigenous cultures recognize psychic abilities in people as a natural part of people's abilities.

As a cautionary note, intuitive people have to take very good care of themselves. When people decided to explore this part of their intuitive awareness they need to be aware of the perils, especially in the early phase of learning. I remember having a warning dream to stay on the very narrow path. It was more than a tight rope, but it was no more than my own width. Attention to being present was the most important aspect of the journey. I remember looking down and all I could see was a giant abyss on both sides of my path, each of the steep sides had no bottom, nothingness all around me. I was warned that I would be tempted to go off the path and fly into the abyss. If I did indeed fly I would be doomed because of a lack of earth beneath my feet. The path was there to help me remember I am a human being and I need the earth's dirt for a strong solid foundation in my training. My simple test was to stay on the path, and the path did lead somewhere. Where was not important, one foot in front of the other was.

When I was a young adult, I heard of people tripping out on LSD acid and never really coming back to their previous self. It might be the same. I do not know. I never did acid. One of my friends told me not to do drugs. He said, "You do not need them. We are trying to get where you are now." We were all seated in a living room visiting and everyone in the room agreed with him. This was way before the cup breaking in my hand. People must have seen something in me that I did not see in myself.

Emotions Can Lower the Vibration

Love is the optimal way of moving to a higher vibration. On an emotional level, love is an action step of doing, not daydreaming, or thinking about "if only". Even if a person does not know what happened in a situation we fill in the gaps with possibilities of the other person's intent, and most often the other's person thoughts and actions are placed in a bad light.

The human condition of fear and self-righteous tunnel vision. Been there, sometimes still do it.

Lower Vibrations has Advantages

Anger and fear are two such emotions. Why? Because it gives us lots of possibilities to understand ourselves better. If we dig a little, we will find a lot about ourselves. Working with our own anger and fear offers an opportunity to understand ourselves and sometimes others better. The old saying about blame—one finger pointing towards the accused and three fingers pointing back. There is much wisdom in this popular adage. We are triggered by something and ask why. We do not always have to know the why. Sitting with your feelings can be just the ticket to open your personal Pandora's Box of memories. Those resentments can goggle up your own happiness. Turning the light onto the hidden feelings, and even just breathing into them can create an opening for more self-love. Let's face it, the world needs more self-love.

In my experience, memories are not always your own. They can be ancestral DNA memories, they can be soul memories, or if you are an empathic energetic sponge they can be other people's feelings. I once cocreated a healing session with a woman who had a weight problem. During the session, her energy field revealed a DNA memory of the idea that she could not lose weight no matter how hard she dieted. This was an ancestor's belief about three or four generations ago. By pulling the ancestral belief about dieting and balancing her chakras, she was able to lose weight. She did join a weight loss group but this time she was successful in her decision to lose weight. She has continued to maintain her weight and commented she is happy with her appearance.

AH HA Moments

I meditated one morning and a thought ended my meditation. I heard my motto is to serve God, the creative divine source of love, and to be of service to people. People, including all aspects of the living earth, part of me has been serving the earth rather than being of service. The earth has been a benign and loving master but my attitude was one of servitude not open-hearted love. It was a way for me to be less intimate with my God/Source, less connected. It created a misaligned boundary in how to interact with others, including the earth. By creating a new healthier boundary with oneself and the creator, a person can feel balanced and stable. Shaming and blaming interfere with your connection. As you know, dogs do better with love rather than shaming and blaming. Dogs want to be love and give love. Creating a god of shame and using the technique of blame—is that not almost blasphemy? To deny our essence of God light and love within us? How can we truly worship God but deny our own spiritual divinity of God's love? If God is the creator of all, would we not always have a heart connection and be connected by the very atoms of the universe. Some say that man makes God in his own image, but if God is everywhere he is much greater than that suggests. God is not a person, but rather an essence of a divine intelligent love vibration. We, as human share this divine love vibration of connection if we chose. Many are called, (we are all called) and few are chosen (we chose ourselves and our divine goodness). We often chose others' wants over our own wants. Acceptance rather than perfection.

More Info about Walk-In Spirits

My Experience: Spirits within Me

Years ago, when I first began to learn about paranormal abilities, I met a couple of women through the internet. One women is an accomplished artist, and is internationally known. I called her Continuum because her psychic abilities seem to go on forever. She was also a biker chick with long painted fingernails. At this time, I was meeting other people who had psychic abilities.

It was through these new acquaintances that I learned about a woman, who used a dowsing tool in her healings. I decided I wanted to learn more about what she did, and booked a session. It was over the phone, no recording. As I remember, she was a retired registered nurse. She had a very soothing caring voice. She began the session and put herself in a meditative state and I was very relaxed. She started asking her spirit guides about me. She told me that her spirit guides had confirmed that I had a number of spirits within me. She said nine. Nine was the number of people living in our childhood home. She told me this was an amazing amount of spirits to be in a person. She felt that their bodies rested in a nearby body of water in Tacoma, and they were not ready to leave the earth. They sought another body. I found out recently either the city or the county dumps unclaimed ashes, and also the corpses of people who are too poor to be able to afford a proper burial into the Commencement Bay in Tacoma, and this has been a long-term practice. Who knew? The energetic worker/healer told me that she was surprised that I had not committed suicide with all those spirits within me. I admitted that I had periodically had suicidal thoughts, but had never had a plan of action. When she said that I realized I did know a number of people in my childhood neighborhood who had had mental health issues or committed suicide. I do not know if they had spirits within them or not and at this point I see no reason to go back in time and find out.

She mentioned it would be hard for me to stay grounded. I mentioned that my nickname was space cadet and people teased me about my spaciness. Once for my Halloween costume I wore a space suit, and braided my long hair into pigtails, and attached two silver helium balloons to the ends of the braids. People understood it immediately and laughed. I was an adult in my late twenties, early thirties. In high school, people teased me about it too. My nickname was Space Cadet. She asked me if I wanted the spirits removed. I said, "Yes please." After the session, I was very grounded, and centered. People now remark about how grounded I am. The spaciness is gone, except the artist's intense creative process. It looks and feels different.

I called my sister. She is nine months older than I am. I told her about the psychic healing session phone call. We both remembered after we moved into that home by the bay we were no longer able to easily talk. We fought all the time, tried to put a line down the middle of our room, but still had lots of fights, to the point that my parents gave us separate rooms. That was pretty amazing when you realize we had nine people in the house and only five bedrooms. So, it must have been that bad. She told me that she felt like she lost her best friend. I was not the same person. After that healing session, we began again to be very close friends. We talk now about once a week or so.

Identifying and Clearing Walk-Ins

After my own experience with walk-ins I was motivated to learn more about them and if possible learn the technique to clear them. For the person that is wondering do they have a spirit inside of them, a few questions asked and answered will be helpful.

First question: Have you ever done something and did not know why? An example of an outburst of anger and it really did not feel like you.

Second question: Have you noticed any changes in your relationship with others?

Third question: Have family and friends commented to you that you seem different?

Fourth question: Have you become noticeably more spacy without any real reason, such as hormones?

Fifth question: Have you had suicidal ideation and wondered almost where it came from? Like an overwhelming need to leave daily life? Yet not really feeling that way.

Walk-ins appear to have a tough time leaving someone's body without assistance or the person dying. Once back in a body they may not enjoy the limits of daily living, and besides it is not the life they left. It is your life. Some people are trained to clear spirits and send them to another dimension in time. It is important to find a qualified person, just like you would for any professional service. Ask people that you trust. Go to New Age bookstores and ask for their recommendations. It really is more about the energetic vibration, but showmanship and ritual is a nice touch. Most of all trust your gut.

A case study: One client had a solid marriage and was deeply in love with her husband. For the first five years, they had a very loving, enjoying and communicative marriage. Something changed for her and tension began to mount in the marriage. She was afraid their relationship was heading for divorce and yet she could not put her finger on the problem. She sought me out to find out if I had any intuitive hints as to the problem. As I talked to her, she told me that at times she did not recognize herself, and her actions even puzzled her. She had no idea why she was doing them. She had had some suicidal thoughts and this was also new. We did a cocreative session and the spirit was released from her body and went to the next level of energetic vibration. Months later she reported she felt like her old self and she and her husband were getting along fabulously.

Ready for a surprise? Not everyone wants their walk-in to leave. Sometimes the walk-in is a childhood friend that has died. Neither one was ready to release the friendship. Others have had a spirit within them for years and feel very lonely without their spirit friend. In these cases, the entity is removed, but the client invites them back again. The difference is they now know and can freely choose. Sometimes a person will come back and ask me to remove the spirit again and yet again. Three times is my limit for removal. My work is a cocreative process not a laundromat.

How does a walk-in enter the body? My understanding is there are a number of ways. One, a tear in the energy field can result in a poor boundary, Two, sleeping with your head pointed in an eastern direction; flying in your sleep can mean you have left your body and an entity can enter when your spirit has left your body. Thirdly, drunkenness and/or being high on drugs can allow your body to be defenseless, and your energy field thin and fragile. Fourth, during a hospital operation. Your energy field is also being operated on by the nature of surgery.

Remember none of these possibilities definitely means you will have a walk-in. If you are aware of the dangers, it is much easier to keep yourself safe. An example is locking your doors in your home. Much less chance of someone coming into your home uninvited. One time I did not see a middle age friend of mine for a long time. I had heard he had had some difficulties with his health and drugs. I was not prepared for what I saw. He reminded me of an unsophisticated 15-year-old teenage girl, just learning about herself. Another friend confirmed she had noticed a change too, and mentioned he had not been the same since a hospital operation he had had. Plus, he had a serious illness and rumors swirled he was using recreational illegal drugs. The good news is the next time I saw him he seemed more like himself.

In my observation people use alcohol and drugs to dull their intuition—and it will. The body receives intuitive information through the chakras. If you have ever known anyone who became addicted to alcohol or drugs they will tell you they often feel alone and isolated. This I-am-isolated feeling can happen if they are in a large group of people or by themselves. Possibly, they have shut down or closed their chakras wheel and are no longer able to connect with others and with God. I have also seen large tarlike substance in the back of people's head, right about the neck. For myself, when I quit drinking alcohol, my intuitive clear vision abilities were greatly enhanced.

Being an intuitive can be very difficult for people. You are susceptible to other people's energy and feelings. You can be feeling terrific and all of a sudden, a person walks by and you feel different, maybe even mad. This can also occur when you are having a heart-to-heart with someone. After the conversation, they feel energized and you feel tired and drained. Did the other person knowingly do that? Most likely not. Sometimes yes. Western culture is becoming more open to paranormal understanding, and we are becoming more interested in the Asian concepts of a Chi force and Feng Shui.

AH HA Moments

This is a repeat idea of an AH HA Moments because it is saying so much. Many are called but few are chosen means we choose our soul path. We have the gift of free will. We are not robots programed to do God's bidding rather we are respected individuals of the cocreative process of living.

My Concluding Remarks

My *Why* has changed slightly as I finish
writing my book.

We all have paranormal encounters. At least,
based on the remarks I hear from people; some almost
in a whisper. It is time for all of us to be more open to
our paranormal experiences. It really is our normal so
let us get over this pretending to ignore it. I know
some people say paranormal experiences are bad and
fearful. Well, I agree with them. Evil exists in all
worlds including the paranormal.   Praying and
surrounding yourself in white light helps. Be aware if
a spirit, or someone is trying to control your behavior.
Love is an action of an open hand, not a closed fist.

Bad and good exist in many realms
including the paranormal world. Love versus evil is
not a linear thought of good and evil. Rather, I see it
more as a spiral energy form of going back and forth
with our thoughts and actions. An example is, joy
versus fear; love versus hate, are moveable feelings,
not stuck on one spectrum point of a spiral diagram.

The heavier our emotions the more difficult it is to seek social interactions. Social interactions are not driven by the number of friends you have, but rather the quality of the friendships.

And finally, people have asked me do I pray a lot. Yes, it helps me stay safe, and balanced in my paranormal world. It keeps my aura sparkling. Meditation, exercise, no drugs or alcohol, reduced caffeine and good nutrition are all important in the energetic working world. Caffeine is my weakness so as I write this I am writing it to myself too. Thank you for sharing my journey and I invite you to go to my suggested reading list for more information.

Also, some of you most likely want to focus on a breathing exercise. Below is an easy task for you to do just that.

Breathe Exercise

Please sit in a chair, nearby have a fresh glass of purified water. You are ready. Take a sip of water. Make sure your feet are flat on the ground and your legs or arms are not crossed. This helps make you a clear connective channel with your surroundings. I want you to take a breath, hold it and release with the sound of OMMMM. Please continue this breath work. *If you start to feel lightheaded stop.* As you do this breath work really feel your body and mind working together. If weather permits go outside and sit on the ground. Remember how your body felt with the breath work and the OMMMM sound. Remember the red root chakra and focus you breathe in the sacrum or tail bone. Too complicated? Okay, sit outside or stand outside, listen to your breath.

Yes, you and the earth are now working together as an energetic team. We really are one. Have fun with it and of course, as a safety feature bubble-up with white light. Have Dazzle Day!

Suggested Reading

Battaglia, Salvatore. *The Complete Guide to Aromatherapy*, Australia, The Perfect Portion, 1997.

The Bhagavad-Gita. Translated by Barbara Stoler Miller, NY NY Bantam Classics, 1986.

Boulder, Russell. Earth Energy Healing (EEH) Website, http://www.earthenergyhealing.org (consulted 1/16/2017).

Chodron, Pema. *When Things Fall Apart*, Boston, MA Shambhala Publications, 1997.

Dalai Lama. *Ethics for the New Millennium*, NY Riverhead Books, Penguin Putnam Inc., 1999.

———. *Awakening the Mind, Lightening the Heart*, NY, NY, HarperCollins, 1995.

———. *The Power of Compassion*, New York, NY, HarperCollins, 1995.

Findhorn Community. *The Findhorn Garden Story*, Findhorn, Scotland 2008.

Ervin, Keith, *Fragile Majesty*, Seattle, The Mountaineers, 1989.

Goodall, Jane. *In the Shadow of Man*, New York, NY, Dell Publisher, 1971.

―――. *The Ten Trusts: What We Must Do to Care for the Animals We Love* (with Marc Bekoff). San Francisco: Harper, 2002.

―――. *Harvest for Hope: A Guide to Mindful Eating* New York: Warner Books, 2005.

―――. *Seeds of Hope: Wisdom and Wonder from the World of Plants* (with Gail Hudson) Grand Central Publishing, 2013.

Hawkins, David, *Letting Go, The Pathway of Surrender, Hays House, Inc., 2014.*

Kenyon, Tom. *Brain States*, Naples, FL., United States Publishing, 1994.

Krieger, Dolores, Ph.D., R.N. *Therapeutic Touch, Inner Workshop*, Santa Fe, New Mexico, Bear and Company, 1997.

Linn, Denise. *Sacred Space*, New York, Ballantine Books, 1995.

Maclean, Dorothy. *Memoirs of an Ordinary Mystic*, Scotland, Lorian, 2010.

McLuhan, T.C. (complied). *Touch the Earth, A Self-Portrait of Indian Existence*, NY, Promontory Press, 1971.

Marquist, Collen and Jack Frasl. *Crystalline Communion*, Vol.1-3, Kirkland, WA. The EarthLight, 1991-1995.

Melody. *Love is in the Earth,* Wheat Ridge, CO Earth-Love Publishing House, 2000.

Pond, David. *Chakras, Beyond Beginners*, Woodbury, MN, Llewellyn, 2016.

—————. *Chakras for Beginners,* St. Paul, MN. Llewellyn, 1999.

Rosenberg, Marshall B., Ph.D. *Nonviolent Communication: A Language of Life* Encinitas, CA: PuddleDancer Press, 2003.

—————. *Speak Peace in the World*, Encinitas, CA: PuddleDancer Press, 2005.

Santo Pietro, Nancy. *Feng Shui, Harmony by Design*, NY, NY, Penguin, 1996.

Scheffer, Mechthild. *Bach Flower Therapy*, Rochester, Vermont, Healing Arts Press, 1988.

Thompkins, Peter, and Christopher Bird. *The Secret Life of Plants*, New York, Avon Books, 1973.

Van Gelder Kunz, Dora. *The Personal Aura,* Wheaton, Ill, Quest Books, 1991.

———, with Dolores Krieger, Ph.D. R.N, (contributor). *The Spiritual Dimension of Therapeutic Touch*, USA, Bear &Company, 2004.

Wohileben, Peter and Tim Flannery. *The Hidden Life of Trees*, Greystone, Books 2016.

Yogananda, Paramahansa. *The Autobiography of a Yogi*, Los Angeles, CA, Self-Realization Fellowship, 1956.

———. *Sayings of Yogananda*, Los Angeles, CA, Self-Realization Fellowship, 1968.

Acknowledgements

I thank my family and friends for their support. I want to thank my clients for cocreating with me in the work. I thank all the people who inspire me to do good in this world. I thank all the peacciors who bring love and kindness. I thank Jane Goodall for being my hero of superb focus. I thank Ellen DeGeneres for her love for dancing, laughter and kindness. I thank all the energetic workers for our earth with a wish for them to be happy and joyous and use their talent to cocreate for others' benefits. I thank all the people who love our earth as much as I do, and want the earth to be honored and healed. Most of all I thank you for reading my book.

Fictitious Names

The names beside my own are fictitious to protect the identities of others. People like their privacy and I want to respect their right to privacy.

Cover Art by Anne Marie/SUMMER

This is a partial photo of a living mandala. Living because I have continued to add paint and materials for the last twenty years. This type of art is called Turn Art™. Why, because it can be hung in assorted directions and the idea is that there is no one way to look at art or life. SUMMER is my artist signature name.

Photos Available on My Website

Photos of my spirit paintings, including a picture of my son and his guardian angel, (no wings on this angel), supernatural beings, outer space scenes and characters, and my pyramid adventure in Chichen-Itza are available for one dollar USD. Yes, it is a playful marketing tool, and a scavenger hunt of sorts. Here is the link to the page.

http://www.cocreatehealth.com/store/c1/Featured_Products.html

About the Author/ Contact Info

Anne Marie McNamara lives in Seattle, WA. She is grateful for her cherished memories. Her indoor plants are her pets and she loves them. She is also blessed with one son, one daughter-in-law and two dazzle grandkids. Her art studio is the best gift she has ever given herself. Someone asked me if I plan to write some more about my adventures? It is a possibility.

The best way to reach Anne Marie for booking an appointment for space clearing for prosperity and joy is through her website: http://www.cocreatehealth.com or email Annemarie@cocreatehealth.com.

If you are interested in viewing more of her art or purchasing her artwork, see http://www.annemariemcnamara.com.

51171376R00131

Made in the USA
San Bernardino, CA
14 July 2017